EDWARDIAN WITNEY

CO – LS

Co	1/03
BU	
SU	11/04

EDWARD VII 1901-1910

EDWARDIAN WITNEY

1901 – 1910

LIFE IN WITNEY BASED ON THE WITNEY GAZETTE

By

CHARLES and JOAN GOTT

MILL HOUSE PUBLICATIONS WITNEY

59 Weavers Close, Witney, Oxfordshire, England.

MMII

Printed by
INFORMATION PRESS
Southfield Road,
Eynsham,
Oxon.

PUBLISHED BY
MILL HOUSE PUBLICATIONS WITNEY.

Copyright © Charles and Joan Gott

ISBN 0 9524405 1 2

ACKNOWLEDGEMENTS

This book is based on items published in the Witney Gazette of 1901-1910, which is available on British Library microfilm (RR16X and RR17X), at Witney Library. All images bearing the initials BL come from this microfilm, and are reproduced by permission of the British Library. We are most grateful to the staff of Witney Library for their friendly help and encouragement during our researches.

The detail of the portrait, King Edward VII, by Sir Luke Fildes, on page 2, is reproduced by courtesy of the National Portrait Gallery, London.

Very special thanks go to Tom Worley for allowing us to reproduce photographs from his extensive collection of local pictures. These appear on pages 9,12,15,20,32,34,38,46 and 64. We are also very grateful to Anne Dossett-Davies for her kind help with the proof-reading, and her valuable comments about layout.

Our thanks go to Paul Cooper for drawing the town map inside the front cover.

INTRODUCTION

This book is based on the Witney Gazette of the early 1900s, which contains a fascinating blend of material. Local news takes up only a page or two, though advertisements for local businesses are spread exuberantly throughout. Local opinion, or a section of it, is taken care of by the thrusting comments of 'Jottings' and the equally eloquent Burford editorialist. Syndicated items include jokes, handy hints and lengthy serial stories with titles such as 'The Mystery of a Hansom Cab', and 'Five Red Marks'. National and international news takes up quite a lot of space: though it is hard to resist lingering over such headlines as 'Suicide in Lion's Cage' or 'Wreck of the Argonaut', such syndicated stories are only included in this book if mentioned by 'Jottings'.

All the events and opinions we have featured come from the Gazette. Sometimes we have simply copied the item word for word, but it has often been necessary to shorten or paraphrase it to save space: journalists in the 1900s expressed themselves much more expansively than they do today.

This is not a scholarly study, but an idiosyncratic choice of material which tends to reflect our own interests. We record events that are very like - or very unlike - things that happen in Witney today; unusual or freakish events; workaday matters and traditional celebrations like Witney Feast. Opinions, too, are important. We have not reproduced a 'Jottings' column, but have often attached the writer's comment to a news item: you will soon be able to recognise him. Where stories of tragedy or crime appear, we have not mentioned names if they could cause distress to present-day families, though, of course, the names are in the original Witney Gazette. Political correctness was unheard-of in Edwardian times; we have not flinched from reproducing some words and opinions which are offensive to many people in the 21st century, including ourselves.

The items are arranged strictly according to the months in which they appear, though we have been a bit more free with some of the advertisements. Our book contains few photographs: the handful found in the Gazette are of very poor quality, and we have included one or two from other sources. We have used place-name spellings as we found them in the Gazette; these are not always consistent (for instance Cogges/Coggs). We have kept pounds, shillings, pence, feet, inches, yards, gallons, hundredweights etc unchanged, but there is a page at the end of the book to help anyone wishing to know more about them.

Practically every item we have chosen invites research, but if we had pursued each one the book would never have been published. So if you want to dig more deeply, just go down to Witney Library, where you can view the old newspapers on microfilm at your leisure. We have thoroughly enjoyed doing just that, and we hope our readers will find interest and amusement in the result.

WITNEY AT THE TURN OF THE CENTURY

What sort of a town was Witney at the beginning of the twentieth century? Certainly a 1901 resident would have no difficulty in recognising the centre of town as it is now, at the beginning of the twenty-first. There have been changes: new roads have been built, some houses pulled down, many private houses have turned into shops, but still the basic plan of West End, Bridge Street, High Street, Market Square, Church Green and Corn Street are much the same. The shops have changed out of all recognition. The biggest difference is that housing estates have been built all around the old core of Witney.

During the 20th century the population of Witney Urban District grew sevenfold. In 1901 there were 3,574 inhabitants; by 2001 the number had risen to about 22,000. The town was small enough in 1901 for everyone to know each other. There were in total 835 houses. The place was hardly more than a large village. Although there were some new houses built between the turn of the century and the Great War, the population had dropped by 45 to 3529 in 1911, according to the census of that year. Most of the new houses were constructed on the New Yatt and Woodstock roads; the wealthier inhabitants built themselves large properties in keeping with their status. While the majority of the dwellings consisted of over four rooms, there were 258 recorded as having fewer than four, and 40 with only two.

The town was only just getting used to being governed by an elected Urban District Council instead of the old Parish Council. The Local Government Act of 1888 had established County Councils, Urban District Councils and Rural District Councils. Local Government does not seem to have been much concerned with party politics; in the County Council election for 1901 all the candidates in the Witney area were returned unopposed, and are the same people as those elected twelve years earlier. No mention is made in the Gazette as to which party they belonged to.

Sanitation was somewhat primitive. Water came from wells: the larger houses would have their own wells and smaller properties would share one with neighbours in the street. Lavatories consisted of earth closets or buckets. Often the earth closets leaked into the wells, contaminating them and causing serious diseases like cholera and typhoid. During 1900 a start was made on putting in a sewage system and a piped water supply. The problems of the sewers seem to have taken up most of the time of the Urban District Council. There were endless crises: the drains in Bridge Street were being laid at the wrong level. Whose fault was it? The contractors were not clearing up the mess they caused in the streets. In the centre of the town the trenches for the pipes had to be so deep (14 feet in Market Square) that they were below the water table and pumps had to run day and night to keep the trenches dry; it also meant that the wells ran dry and water had to be taken round in a horse-drawn water cart.

The Council was also involved in the improvement of Church Green, which had become very rutted and eroded. The level of the Green was raised by eight feet, using the extra earth from digging the sewer trenches. This caused endless rows among the councillors about allowing the fair at Witney Feast to take place on the expensively transformed Green.

The motorcar hardly existed in Witney, though in the Gazette of 1900 there is mention of a motor travelling too fast in Corn Street. This may have been the only one in town. For several years after this, cars rarely figure in the news; their absence, however, did not mean the absence of accidents. There were many cases of horses bolting, carts and traps getting smashed, and people suffering cuts, bruises or at the worst broken bones. Fatalities were rare. The police came down heavily on anyone caught driving a cart without lights, and drunk driving was also a serious offence. The roads were not tarred, but had a metalled surface consisting of compacted stone which had to be rolled regularly by steamroller. During the summer dust settled on the roads, and the Council would send out a water cart to sprinkle them. In wet weather mud was the problem - and horse dung had to be contended with at any time.

Trains were an important means of transport: the Witney railway ran from Fairford to Oxford, providing five trains a day in each direction. The journey from Witney to Oxford took 30 minutes. Passengers arriving in Witney would find Paine's horse-drawn bus waiting for them outside the station.

The richer people of the town had gas installed in their homes for cooking and lighting. It came from Witney's own gas-works, which stood in what is now the Waitrose car park. Gas was also used for lighting in the factories, where incandescent mantles were taking the place of the open (fishtail) flame as the source of light. In 1901 electricity was just coming to the town, provided by the Witney Electric Supply Company. The UDC was talking about changing from gas to electric street lighting, but this did not happen until many years later.

Although Witney was famous both at home and abroad for the quality of the blankets made in its mills, it was also a thriving market town providing for the needs of an agricultural community. There were businesses like Leigh & Son, who sold farm machinery, and there were blacksmiths who not only acted as farriers but also mended implements and carts for the farmers.

Every other Thursday, cattle, sheep, pigs and chickens were sold in the Market Square. The mess, noise and smell in the town centre on market days must have been formidable, with trails of dung in the streets left by animals being walked in from nearby farms or from the railway station, and the shouts of the vendors and buyers mingling with the grunts, bleats and moos of the merchandise. Occasionally a cow would run amok and charge off down the High Street. Selling began with the sheep, just after the arrival of the 12.45 train from Oxford. There were special cheap day tickets to Witney on market days. Most of the public houses near Market Square would remain open until 4pm on Thursdays, to satisfy the farmers' thirst.

The town had two large department stores: Cook & Boggis, Cash Drapers and Clothiers, and Valentine & Barrell, which sold everything from clothes to perambulators. It also had a brewery, Clinch & Co, which owned most of the public houses, having bought out the other smaller breweries. There were 35 licenced premises, one for roughly every hundred men, women and children, made up of 24 public houses, eight beer taverns and three shops. Comments in the Witney Gazette suggest that many people thought this was too many. The town also had its own bank, Gilletts, which at the turn of the century printed its own notes.

Education was compulsory and free up to either the age of twelve or to passing Standard 4. This was raised to Standard 5 in 1901. Many parents were taken to court for failing to send their children to school regularly. The main schools were the National School (St Mary's) on Church Green, the Wesleyan School near the Wesleyan Chapel and the Blue Coat School, a charity school set up for the sons of blanket weavers. There were also a few privately run schools. Secondary education, which in most cases had to be paid for, was either at the Grammar School (Henry Box), which had only 12 pupils in 1900, or the Technical School. In 1901 these two schools were amalgamated.

Religion - and the social events organised by the various churches - played an important part in the lives of Witney townspeople. At St Mary's, the hardworking and popular Canon Foxley Norris was nearing the end of his 25 years as Rector. The Wesleyan Chapel had a large congregation, and the Wesleyan school was flourishing. Congregationalists, Friends and Primitive Methodists all had their following.

In the wider world, the second Boer War was raging in South Africa. The sieges of Ladysmith, Kimberley and Mafeking, as well as the Boers' victory at Spion Kop in January 1900 were serious defeats for the British troops, but soon afterwards their fortunes began to change. Several Witney men were among those fighting for their country.

Saint Mary's Church

HER MAJESTY QUEEN VICTORIA
1837 – 1901

1901

The year starts with the death of Queen Victoria. She had reigned for 63 years. When the news reached Witney there was confusion as to whose job it was to read the proclamation of the new king. Should it be the Bailiffs or the Urban District Council? There was nobody about who remembered the previous occasion in 1842, and at that time elected councils did not exist and the Bailiffs ran the town. Some of the councillors were away at the time and hasty meetings were called to organise the event. It was decided that the senior Bailiff should read the proclamation from a white horse.

The Urban District Council was still concerned about the sewers and the new water supply. At most meetings of the Council there was some problem about the contractors, about the mess caused, or about the noise of the pumps to keep the water level down in the trenches. Why was the drilling of the borehole at Apley Barn going so slowly? Would the borehole provide enough water? What was it all going to cost and did the town really need a sewage system? In spite of these problems, the ratepayers seem not unduly concerned as most councillors were returned unopposed in the March Council election.

The amalgamation of the Grammar School with the Blue Coat charity School caused some dissension and numerous letters to the Gazette.

England, led by a Conservative Liberal Unionist Coalition under Lord Salisbury, was at war in South Africa and also in China, where the Boxer Rebellion against foreigners was smouldering on, finally to end in September with the signing of the peace protocol on September 7th. In South Africa the British troops were slowly getting the upper hand, while at home there was considerable opposition to the policy of rounding up all Boer families and putting them into "concentration camps". "Jottings" was urging more young men to volunteer to go to the war.

The beginning of the women's suffrage movement was making itself felt, but at this stage the Gazette has nothing to say on the matter.

NEW YEARS EVE SERVICE

The passing of the old year was marked with a service in St Mary's church at 8 o'clock in the evening. On January 1st it was back to work as usual.

BREAD FOR ALL

As usual at this time of year the Waring charity was distributed in the Corn Exchange. All the poor of Witney and some of the not so poor should give thanks to Elijah Waring who in 1813 directed £1000 to be given to Witney; the interest was to be applied for the purchase of bread to be distributed among the poor inhabitants of Witney, Hailey, Crawley and Newland. In all 2089 loaves were given away.

LUCKY ESCAPE

A little girl called Harris travelling on the morning train from Southleigh to Witney fell out of the moving train. She had been playing with the handle of the door at the time. When the train arrived at Witney station the stationmaster was told. He immediately rushed back along the track and found the little girl unhurt.

12th NIGHT PARTY

As is the custom a great party was held in the Corn Exchange to mark the end of the Christmas festivities. The children had the hall from 5pm till 10 o'clock, and then it was the turn of the adults to enjoy themselves with dancing and merrymaking till 2 in the morning.

QUEEN VICTORIA IS DEAD

The Queen passed away on January 22nd at 6 in the evening. Her family were by her bedside at Osborne House on the Isle of Wight. The funeral will take place on February 2nd.

PROCLAMATION OF KING EDWARD VII AT THE BUTTER CROSS , WITNEY

The proclamation of the new King was first read by the town Bailiff seated on a white charger, from outside Staple Hall. The Bailiff, the Council and many townsfolk processed to Corn Street where the proclamation was again read, with a third reading by the Butter Cross.

****

CHANGE IN SCHOOL LEAVING RULES

The Government has decreed that children may only leave school before the age of 12 if they have passed standard 5 instead of at present being allowed to leave on passing standard 4.

STREET LIGHTING

Although nobody in Witney wants to pay more in rates, is it really necessary only to have the streetlights on when there is no moon? Often even on nights of a full moon it is cloudy and unsafe to walk in the streets at night.

THE QUEEN'S FUNERAL

All businesses in the town closed on Saturday for the funeral of the Queen. On the Friday afternoon the firing of the cannons from the ships in the channel could be quite distinctly heard as the Queen's coffin was brought from the Isle of Wight to Southampton.

THE KING OPENS HIS FIRST PARLIAMENT

On February 14th, Saint Valentine's Day, King Edward VII opened his first parliament.

A DISGRACE

The road to Curbridge is again in a most wretched state. Pedestrians who must take the road as there is no footpath have to wade through ankle deep. As County Councillors are now seeking re-election it would not be a bad plan for the Curbridge people to get their representative to walk along that road, and then ask him his opinion; it is certainly nothing short of a disgrace to the County Council to refuse the reasonable request of the people of the village for a decent footpath.

TUCKERS' FEAST

The annual dinner of Tuckers employed by Messrs C. Early & Co. took place in the Temperance Hotel on Shrove Tuesday. Mr. C. Early presided, supported by C.W. Early, J.V. Early, J. H. Early and Gerald Early. After the loyal toasts, the health of Mr Gerald Early of Mafeking was enthusiastically received. A pleasant time was afterwards spent in various games, vocal music etc. Mr and Mrs Dring catered in their usual satisfactory manner.

THE TUCKER'S SONG

The wondrous globe on which we live
Is quite surrounded everywhere
With something quite invisible
It's called the atmospheric air.
The air is fluid light and thin,
Which forms of gas it does combine;
It carries sound in order well
When put in motion it is wind.

Chorus
Oh! how curious, wonderfully curious,
The laws of Nature are indeed
Most wonderfully curious.

The wondrous globe on which we live
The seaman spreads his canvas sail
And as he moves on quick or slow
He calls it breeze, or storm, or gale.
But when it blows with so much power
Till all resistance is in vain
Blowing at eighty miles an hour
He calls it then a Hurricane.

Chorus

The winds, the seas the tempest blown
Are very changeable indeed,..
But in the torrids they are known
One way for six months doth proceed,
Oft does the wind make ruins lie,
But their usefulness has been understood,
For in the Bible we are told
God guides the wind and rules the flood.

Chorus

The Medical Health officer, Mr W. D. Hyde, reported that the health of the town had been very good over the past year with a scarcity of infectious diseases. This was largely due to most of the town being supplied with water from the well on Church Green. Many of the private wells were very polluted.

	1900	1899	Notifiable disease 1900
Deaths (All)	69	65	Diphtheria 2
Under 1 year	8	17	Whooping cough 2
Under 5 years	5	23	Consumption 5
Under 17 years	5	6	Pneumonia 6
			Heart disease 10
Births	66	106	

NO CHANGE IN COUNCIL

County Council nominations were made on Thursday and almost all the old members were returned unopposed. In the Witney and Hailey division Messrs W. Smith and J. V. Early who have represented the district since the County Council was formed 12 years ago have been re-nominated with no opposition. The people of the district are to be congratulated on having such able gentlemen to represent them. In the U.D.C. Messrs Batt, Bartlett, Early and Tarrant were nominated, as there were no other nominations they have been re-elected.

SUMMONED BEFORE THE GUARDIANS

John Long of Brighthampton was summoned by the Witney Guardians of the Workhouse to show cause why he should not pay 2s a week maintenance for his father who was a charge on the Union Workhouse. Long, who was unmarried and lived rent-free, said he earned 11s a week. He paid 2s for Firing (*Fuel),* 1s washing. If he paid 2s for his father's keep this would only leave him 6s to live on. He was ordered to pay 1s a week and 8s costs.

THE END OF THE BLUE COAT SCHOOL

The Charity Commission has suggested a scheme to close the Blue Coat School, a charity originally set up in 1723 by John Holloway to provide an education and apprenticeships for the sons of poor journeymen in the blanket industry. Now that there is free education for all to the age of 12 years, there is no need for such a charity. The Charity Commission suggests that the Grammar School founded by Henry Box and the Technical School should be combined to form one school, the Witney Grammar and Technical School. The Charity Commissioners' scheme was to use the money from the Blue Coat School to provide scholarships for blanket workers to the new combined school.

A **public meeting** was held in the Corn Exchange to protest at the Charity Commission's scheme. The meeting was well supported by the owners of the Blanket Mills. A resolution was passed by the meeting that the money should be spent on:
1. Apprenticeship fees or scholarships according to parental choice.
2. Clothing for the apprentices and scholarship pupils.

AN ACCIDENT

On Thursday afternoon a horse and trap belonging to Mr Henry Shayler of Minster Lovell was in the High Street, when the horse in some way took fright and galloped up the street colliding with a heavy cart loaded with potatoes belonging to Mr Michael Pratley of Hailey. The collision also involved a small trap belonging to Mr Robinson, of New Yatt. In the latter two persons were seated. One was thrown out but happily received no injury. The only damage done was to Mr Shayler's trap, the shafts were smashed to atoms and the wheels torn from it, and considerably damaged. Many people were in the street at the time and considerable excitement prevailed.

EASTER CONCERT

A concert is to be held in the Corn Exchange on Easter Monday. There will be a display of animated pictures of Queen Victoria's funeral.

****

A THUNDERBOLT FALLS

A sudden thunderstorm over Witney brought not only peals of thunder, vivid lightning flashes, torrents of rain and large hailstones, but a thunderbolt which fell close to New Mill. It greatly alarmed those in and around the mill with its terrific noise resembling the roar of cannon, and smashed several mill windows. We hear of no further damage.

LIBERAL WOMEN

Speaking to the Witney branch of the Mid Oxfordshire Women's Liberal Association on why she was a Liberal, Miss Maclaren Ramsey said that the Liberals had done more than any other party to extend the franchise, and she believed that through them women would get the right to vote. There was but a small attendance.

POACHERS FINED

Albert Rowles and Edwin Winfield, labourers of Witney and Ducklington, pleaded guilty to Trespass on land in the occupation of John Castle at Ducklington, and were fined 10s each. George Batts, gamekeeper, of Cokethorpe, described seeing them working the rabbit holes in Mr Castle's field with a ferret and two dogs. On seeing him they ran away, leaving the ferret.

THE COST OF A NEW WEATHERCOCK

As reported in the Witney Gazette in December of last year the weathercock was blown off the steeple of Saint Mary's Church. A steeplejack has inspected the spire and estimated the cost at about £360. An eminent architect corroborates the estimate but adds some of the work does not need doing for 30 years. It appears from a report of the Vestry meeting that the authorities are to proceed with all the work at once. Many of the citizens of the town are asking, do we need to spend all this money now to repair the spire, which has nothing to do with a new weathercock?

EASTER SPORTS

Bank Holiday Monday was not favoured by desirable weather. In spite of this 2250 people turned out to watch the sports. Two special trains from Oxford deposited a host of visitors at mid-day.

GREATER COMFORT AT THE WORKHOUSE

In accordance with a circular from the Local Government Board the Guardians of the Witney Union Workhouse have formulated a scheme for the over 65s.
The 12 female inmates over 65 have had their day room made more comfortable by the addition of cushions for the chairs. They are to be allowed tea, sugar and milk with bread and butter or cake in the afternoon. They are also to be allowed to rise an hour later. With regard to the men, of whom there are 35 over 65 the committee stated they required more time before making any definite decisions. Suggestions included an allowance to men over 60 of 1oz of tobacco (per week) instead of ½oz; greater facilities for visits from friends such as walking in the garden for up to half an hour. Visitors from Witney can visit friends twice weekly Tuesdays and Fridays 2 - 4pm. Others may come on any day between 9am and 5pm in case of necessity. All adult inmates will, on application to the master, be permitted leave of absence in uniform or otherwise on the following days:
Males Tuesday and Thursday, Females Wednesday and Friday.
9 to 6 April to September. 9 to 4 October to March.

HIGH STREET FIRE

The Barnes family of 72 High Street, adjoining the King's Head, miraculously escaped death when fire broke out at their home. The alarm was raised at 3.30am by Mr Green, confectioner and baker. With extraordinary presence of mind Mr George Barnes threw out bedding from the front window onto the pavement, then dropped his children onto it. He and his wife escaped down ladders provided by the drainage workers. Mr Dring and other neighbours worked hard to contain the fire with buckets of water until the Fire Brigade under the command of Mr F.M. Green crossed Messrs Lockett's yard to reach the river. The good supply of water from the hoses soon mastered the flames, though the staircase was burnt to a cinder.

HEROS' RETURN

2nd VOLUNTEER BATTALION OXFORDSHIRE LIGHT INFANTRY ARRIVE IN SOUTHAMPTON RETURNING FROM THE SOUTH AFRICAN WAR.

The Bailiffs had intended to give a Dinner to honour the returning volunteers to Witney. When it was realised that there were only two from Witney, Corporal John Scanes and Corporal Leo Whitcher, the idea was abandoned. Instead it was agreed that a watch should be presented to each of them, engraved as follows

South African War
1900-01
Presented to
Name
The 2nd Vol. Bat. O.L.I.
On his return
by the habitants of Witney
as a mark of
their appreciation.

The volunteers arrived in Southampton early in the morning and left at 10.30 by special train arriving in Oxford at 12.30. All the volunteers were taken to the Town Hall for lunch and speeches.

F. Company arranged for a carriage to bring John Scanes and Leo Whitcher from Oxford to Witney. The carriage arrived at the bottom of Cogges Hill promptly at 8pm, and was met by a crowd of over 1000 well-wishers. The horses were removed from the carriage which was then drawn by F Company through the town to the Market Place. By the time it reached the market the crowd had swollen to 3000.

Watches were presented to Scanes and Whitcher by the Rector, with the Bailiffs W. Brooks and C. P. Saltmarsh in attendance. After a speech by the Rector and the singing of the National Anthem, the carriage was drawn to the Cross Keys Hotel for a Smoking Concert given by Captain Ravenor. The evening ended at 11pm when Scanes and Whitcher were carried shoulder high to their homes.

Death of George Hudson

The death has occurred of a very old townsman, George Hudson of the Nelson Inn, Witney, who died on Wednesday last week. The deceased highly respected by all who knew him, was the oldest Licensed Victualler in town having had a licence since 1853. For 35 years he also carried out the business of a butcher.

TROUBLE AT THE MILL

Eliza Rowles a weaver of Witney was summoned by Messrs C. Early and Co. for leaving work without proper notice thereby causing damage to the extent of £1-4s-0d.

Mr Fisher for the prosecution said the sum of £1-4s-0d was not of great moment. The question to be decided was whether there was a well-established custom in the business that a fortnight's notice should be given and received. Eliza Rowles had worked for the company for eleven years weaving on an eighteen quarter loom earning good money. She asked for a bigger loom, expecting to earn more money. She was moved to a larger one when one became available. The defendant said she found the loom she was given was too heavy and she told the foreman she could not manage it. She told him she should leave and offered to serve her time on the old loom. The foreman (A. Hemingway) told her to leave at once.

Abraham Hemingway deposed: Eliza Rowles said, "I can't get on with this loom". I asked her if she had a man to look at it, and she said she had, and that she should not work the loom any longer. I said "You know the remedy, give 14 days' notice"; she replied "I shall not give a minute's notice".

Several witnesses were asked if they remembered a case where a fortnight's notice was not given. None of the witnesses could give an example of leaving without notice, except Ada Wharton who stated that she had left the plaintiff's employ because she was not well, and did not give notice. The Magistrates retired and on their return the chairman said they gave for the plaintiffs.

The prosecution stated that the plaintiffs did not wish the defendant to pay costs. The object of the case was to obtain a definite confirmation that a fortnight's notice had to be given.

A fortnight was allowed for the defendant to pay £1-4s-0d.

HOLLOWAY CHARITY

The proposed amendment to the scheme dealing with the Holloway charity should be satisfactory to the whole town and especially to those for whose benefit the charity was founded. £150 per annum is to be devoted to their benefit exclusively. This will work out at nearly £50 more than they have received before, including apprenticeship fees and clothing.

The basis of the scheme would close the Blue Coat School and merge Witney Grammar School with the Technical Institute to form the Witney Grammar and Technical School. It is laid down that of income accruing to the new school from the Blue Coat School, £150 is to be set aside for the exclusive benefit of children of workmen engaged in the Blanket trade. The money is to be used in the following ways:

Scholarships in the Witney Grammar and Technical School, to be called Holloway and Wright Scholarships.

Apprenticeships for boys and girls in some useful trade or occupation.

To provide boys and girls with outfits on starting work.

A further £50 was set aside to provide a pension for Mr George Owens, the former Master of the Blue Coat School. These changes should take place in 1902. At present the Grammar school has 16 pupils.

PETTY SESSIONS
THEFT OF CIGARETTES.

Walter Grant aged 16, living at 24 Cape Terrace, was charged with stealing one packet of cigarettes

value one shilling the property of Messrs W.H.Tarrant.
. Walter Grant pleaded guilty and was ordered to pay 14 shillings costs.

****

THE NEW WEATHERCOCK

The necessary repairs to the steeple have been completed by Messrs Green and Sons. They have placed a new weather vane. The cock, which measures 31 inches from beak to tail and 22 inches deep, is made of copper beaten thin with 4 coats of leaf gold. Inside the bird has been placed a copy of the Witney Parish Magazine and the Witney Gazette, and a parchment containing the names of the Rector, Church Wardens and committee under whose supervision the work was carried out. The cock was made by Henry Long and Son.

WITNEY TRIP

The trip committee decide that the trip this year should be to Portsmouth on July 16th.

PARKING PROBLEMS

Farmers have been told by an officer of the Council that they may not park their wagons and carts on Church Green on Market days as they have always done in the past. It appears that the officer was over zealous and that the Urban District Council has only prohibited parking on the grassed areas of the Green. They may park on the Macadamised northern end of the Green. Last year the Council spent a considerable amount of money improving the Green which had become deeply rutted and muddy. In fact the level of the Green had to be raised by eight feet. The Council having spent so much effort to get the Green in good condition; wish to keep it this way.

A Witney shower was falling fast
As up the High Street slowly
passed
A man who bore in grasp of ice
An iron sign with this strange
device
KEEP OFF THE GRASS.

SCHOOL TREAT

Wesleyan Day and Sunday School children met on Woodgreen at 2pm. Headed by a band, the school banner, the minister and the school committee, the children marched to St. Mary's Close, which had been placed at their disposal by Dr. Kelly. The children in their dresses and with flags flying presented a pretty appearance. Swings, cricket, rounders and various games were indulged in till 4pm when tea was

served, the children being waited on by their teachers.

After an enjoyable meal games were resumed with renewed vigour, racing and scrambling being the most popular pastimes. At dusk a very pleasant day was brought to an end by fireworks and votes of thanks.

FIRE PRECAUTIONS

For the protection of life and property from fire the Fire Brigade has set up a hand pump with hose, lifeline and fire buckets beneath the Town Hall. The space devoted to this purpose is open as in case of need the appliance will be easily obtainable.

KNIGHT BROS
COAL MERCHANTS
WITNEY

BL

BORING OLD POMPEY AGAIN

The annual trip was as usual enjoyed by everyone. Although Portsmouth is very popular, Portsmouth two years running is a bit much.

WITNEY ANNUAL TRIP

The Committee have made arrangements with the G.W.R. to run a

SPECIAL TRAIN

TO

PORTSMOUTH

ON

TUESDAY, JULY 16TH 1901.

STEAMBOAT TRIPS

To ISLE of WIGHT, TOTLAND, ALUM BAY, SOUTHAMPTON, &c.

DAY FARE from all Stations 5/6.

	4 DAYS	7 DAYS	11 or 14 DAYS
FAIRFORD LECHLADE ALVESCOTT BAMPTON	8/6	9 -	12/0
WITNEY SOUTHLEIGH	8/-	8/6	11/-
EYNSHAM YARNTON	8/-	8/6	10/6

The Train will leave Fairford 4-35, Lechlade 4-48, Alvescott 4-51, Bampton 4-58, Witney 5-14, Southleigh 5-20, Eynsham 5-27, Yarnton 5-35 ; arriving at Portsmouth about 9 a.m.

Return Train will leave Portsmouth Town Station 8-25 p.m.

Passengers holding long period Tickets must return on July 19th, 22nd, or 29th, by the 9-5 a.m. Train from Portsmouth Town Station.

TICKETS must be taken early as only a limited number will be used. The Committee will attend the Corn Exchange, Witney, on Saturday, July 13th, 6-30 p.m. to 9-30 p.m. for the sale of Tickets.

Parties of 8 can have compartments reserved by giving notice on Saturday, July 13th.

W. H. TARRANT & F. M. GREEN, Hon. Secs.

BL

DRUNKENNESS

John Cripps licensed victuallar was summoned by police for permitting drunkenness on a licensed premises. Albert Edward Florey of Newland, carpenter, deposed that on Sunday 30th June, "I went to the Carpenter's Arms at 12.30 and remained till 2pm. I had 5 or 6 pints of beer. There were others in the tap room. I was drunk when I left the house. When I got home my mother helped me in-doors and I went to sleep till 4.30. I went back to the Carpenter's Arms at 6 o'clock and remained till twenty minutes to nine, I had about 5 pints. The landlady served me. About 8 o'clock the landlady told me my father was outside. I was very drunk. The landlady supplied me with more beer after 8 o'clock. I left at twenty minutes to nine and found my father outside. My father helped me home and being helplessly drunk my father and mother put me to bed. It must have been clear to the landlady that I was helplessly drunk."

The bench imposed a fine of £3 on the landlord saying the magistrates considered it a bad case, but they had taken into consideration it was a first offence.

WITNEY GAS AND COKE COMPANY

At the Annual General Meeting of the Witney Gas and Coke Company it was reported that the year had been one of progress. One million more cubic feet of gas had been sold this year, an increase of 14%. The number of slot meters in use had increased by 49 to 129, and 174 gas cooking stoves were in use. The directors advised a dividend of 3% for the half year making 5% for the year.

Today's telegram

Proclamation to the Boers

Lord Kitchener's latest proclamation warns the Boer leaders that unless they surrender before 5th September they will be permanently banished from South Africa. Burghers are warned that unless they surrender the cost of maintaining their families will be charged against their property.

FATHER TO PAY

A labourer of Northmoor was summoned by a young woman of the same village to show cause why he should not contribute towards the support of her child, of whom she alleged he was the father. The defendant acknowledged the paternity, and an order was made upon him to pay 1s 6d a week and 8s costs.

URBAN DISTRICT COUNCIL

The Council discussed the question of protecting the newly restored Church Green from the damage done by the Witney Feast Fair.
Also discussed was the amount of street lighting that should be left on all night during the winter months. The Council recommended that the following lights should remain lit all night: Bridge Street (Mr Fowler's), the Bridge High Street (Mr Tite's), G.P.O., Market Square (Alfred L. Leigh), Corn Street (Parliament House) and the corner of Lowell's Yard. All the lights to be extinguished at 10 o'clock. The lamp-lighter should start at Wood Green and finish at the Leys, so as there is light till the last train has gone.

ALARMING FIRE AT BRIDGE STREET MILL

At a quarter to seven on Friday morning, fire broke out in the willying room at Bridge Street Mill, and had it not been for the promptitude of members of the firm and some of their employees, a serious outbreak must have occurred. The room was in flames in a moment, and within a few seconds the steam whistle was sounded, and many willing hands were throwing water at the flames. On hearing the whistle Herbert Smith immediately ran to the fire engine station, and by the time some of the Brigade arrived the engine was in readiness for use. Within five minutes of the alarm sounding the engine arrived on the scene of the conflagration; by this time the flames were getting hold of the roof, while inside the room was a sheet of flame. Fortunately the doors connecting this room with other parts of the factory are of iron and consequently the flames were confined to this department. Within three quarters of an hour the flames were extinguished, but not before considerable damage had been done; one man working in the room at the time received several burns, and the machinery in the room was rendered unfit for use, the damage being estimated at £500.

****

******

*

WITNEY FEAST

For the first time the fair was not held on Church Green; although caravans were allowed to be drawn upon the lawns in front of the houses on the west side of the green, up as far as the Limes. The roadway from the bottom of the Hill to the Bull Inn was blocked to general traffic, this being diverted behind the forge past the Corn Exchange to the station.

Stalls and shows reached from the Post Office to the Bull. This arrangement was very cramped and received much adverse criticism, and probably would have been more severely condemned had not the rain come on and dispersed the thousands which were filling up the narrow gangway early in the afternoon of the Monday. In the roadway just opposite the Brewery was Bailey's celebrated switchback, which as usual did a roaring business for young and old. Next followed the Galloping Horses which with cocoa-nut and bowling spaces reached to the entry to Corn Street. The centre of the Market Square was entirely occupied by the show of Messrs Taylor and A. Ball. The Cinematograph is indeed a very popular exhibition. There were some splendid local views including a view of Church Green with school boys at drill. There is a word of commendation to the proprietors of the show. All the pictures exhibited were of the most refined character and there was the total absence of anything at all objectionable. There were of course the inevitable peepshow and multiscope, but apparently business was not very brisk with them.

The last but by no means the least feature of the fair was the number of purveyors of fried fish and hot sausages with roast potatoes; there must have been nearly a dozen of these concerns, doing their level best to satisfy the hungry multitude.

THE WITNEY INSTITUTE

The opening of the new Witney Institute is a boon for the working classes of the town (and we all more or less belong to that class). We have heard some fears expressed as to the new Institute injuring the other two places of a similar kind in the town [The *Athenaeum Room* and the *Young Men's Social Club*]. The Institute was opened on Sunday. It is one of which any town could be proud, and is to be found at 52 High Street. The house has been put in good repair and decorated throughout by Jas. Hawood in a style that leaves nothing to be desired. The club is based on the broadest lines. It is unsectarian and non-political, two most important factors in the success of any public institution in a small town like Witney.

Coming to the building itself, we find on entering a well-furnished hall and on the right a commodious and well-ventilated smoke room, where various games can be played. On the left of the hall is the reading room with the principal daily and weekly newspapers and periodicals. Upstairs is the bagatelle room furnished with a new table and the necessary requisites. The billiard room is an exceptionally good one with plenty of light. On three sides of the room are raised platforms for spectators. Leading off this are to be found the lavatory and committee rooms.

WORKHOUSE DRAINS

The amount required by the Witney Urban Council for taking the Workhouse sewage into the new town sewage system is £40 or something like 6 shillings per annum for each person. It is not for us to say whether this is the lowest sum at which the council can undertake the business but we doubt if the Rural Council will consider it "reasonable". There is apparently ample room in the grounds of the Workhouse for the treatment of sewage. If the Rural Council have £40 per annum to spare it would go a good way towards their share of maintaining an isolation hospital which is badly needed by both the Rural and Urban Council.

SEWAGE AGAIN

Will the sewers ever be finished? The sewers in Mill Street have been laid at the wrong depth. Who is to blame? The engineer says he cannot accept the contractors' explanation as to the gradient of the sewer and in the same letter he states he does not consider the contractors to blame. So who is to blame?

LETTER FROM THE FRONT

The following letter has been received by Mr. J. Goves, of the Crofts, Witney:-

```
2nd. Bat Grenadier Guards,
8th Division, Field Force,
South Africa.
      September 21st 1901
```

Dear Mother and Father, Just a few lines hoping they will find you all in good health, as I am pleased to say it leaves me the same. I was pleased to get two letters and two papers from you yesterday when we came in. We went out for a few days along the Drakensberg Range, rounding up cattle and sheep. The first 5 days were the worst I have had since I have been in the country. We went out on out-post duty the first night from here on top of Steynaberg Kopji. The wind was blowing and it was bitterly cold. We had no tents with us; it was terrible. The next day the sun never showed once the whole day. The wind was still blowing a hurricane that night, it was too cold to sleep, and it was dark as pitch. We could not get up and walk about as we could not see where we were going. The next day we found a large cave full of clothing, women's things, about £2000 worth altogether. That night we went on out-post duty again, and the wind was colder still, no sleep again. The next day the wind abated a little, and the rain commenced. I got wet through 3 times, so for 5 nights I was without sleep. Notwithstanding the cold weather &c, we made some wonderful big captures of cattle and sheep, On the 18th we went out in 2 columns. A column escorted the convoy to the next camp; B column made a detour to the right and surrounded 18 Boers, who surrendered. A rather peculiar coincidence occurred on the 18th of this month, it was exactly 18 months since we left England, we trekked exactly 1800 miles to that camp, we captured 18 Boers and 1800 head of mixed cattle, so the 18th is a red letter day. During the 9 days trek our total captures were 3 Reaping machines, 1652 sacks of grain, 15 wagons, 20 ploughs, 11 Cape Carts, 114 Refugee families, 6000 bundles Wheat Straw, 2 Vehicles, 250 Trek Oxen, 4030 Goats, 1502 Cattle, 401 Horses, 4050 Sheep, 28 Boer Riding Horses, 13500 rounds small arm Ammunition, 23 Prisoners, and 24 Rifles, so we did not do badly. I think this is all the news this time, so close with love to all.

I remain your ever-loving Son,

FRANK.

A WIN FOR CURBRIDGE

As has been reported before, the residents of Curbridge have for a long time been trying to persuade the County Council of the need of a footpath from Witney to Curbridge. The County Council has agreed that a footpath should be constructed at the side of the main road leading from Witney to Curbridge at an estimated cost of £50 on condition that the sum of £20 is contributed locally.

EYNSHAM MAN CONVICTED

It is not too much to say that Eynsham once more breathes freely. A labourer from there who got 12 years at the assizes had become the terror of the whole neighbourhood. He was charged with breaking and entering the dwelling house of a 71-year-old widow, between the hours of 12 midnight and 1am on the 10th September with the intent to commit a felony there in Eynsham. He was further charged with feloniously ravishing and carnally knowing her. It is a sad comment on these days of education and enlightenment to find a young man of 28 has been convicted 17 times and now has been sentenced for what the Judge termed the worst offence of its kind he had ever tried. The neighbours rejoiced that for a long time they will be free from the presence of one who is regarded with the utmost loathing.

****

NIGGER ENTERTAINMENT

On Tuesday last the Witney Nigger Troupe gave an entertainment in the Corn Exchange. There was a crowded house to hear the performance, which consisted of comic and sentimental songs etc, most of which were well received. The bad behaviour of a certain portion of the audience prevented many from enjoying the entertainment, and we suggest that at the next performance the presence of a policeman would prevent the repetition of the rowdyism experienced on this occasion.

MR SANTOS DUMONT AND HIS FLYING MACHINE

Mr Santos Dumont, who has been paying a visit to this country, has expressed his view on the future utility of aerial craft. Having solved the problems of aerial flight he intends to put his marvellous discovery to practical use. A journey through the air across the Mediterranean is one of the early items on his programme, and eventually to cross the Atlantic. If Mr Dumont's views prove correct then we may expect aerial navigation to produce a revolution in the present condition of the world. We tremble to think of the airship as an engine of destruction, and the awful effects such a craft would be capable of producing upon humble individuals on Terra-firma are incalculable.

****

GAS-WORKS ON FIRE

Great excitement was caused in Market Square and High Street soon after midnight on Friday 27th when it was discovered the Gas-works were in full blaze. The fire started in the governor-house. The Brigade soon got the flames well in hand and prevented them from spreading to the retort-house, where much greater damage might have been done. The cause of the fire was an escape of gas from the governor, which filled the governor-house. As a gas jet is always kept burning there, an explosion followed which set the whole building in flames. The governor was destroyed and thus the gas from a six-inch pipe was set free to feed the flames until checked by the valve of the holder being closed.

The fire did not seriously affect the supply of gas, which was turned on again at 8 o'clock on Friday morning.

OXFORD TEAM FOR ENGLISH CUP

All lovers of football will be glad to know that the Oxford team is now included in the list of those playing for the English Cup. They have been drawn to play Lincoln, and as Oxford has the choice of ground they will undoubtedly elect to play on their own. There will probably be a big crowd to support our county team when the contest comes off next month.

BEER IN BOTTLES
Parliamentary Act for the New Year

A new Act forbids the sale of intoxicating liquors to children under the age of 14 unless it is sold in corked and sealed bottles, in quantities not less than a pint. It is generally thought that the Act was passed for the promotion of temperance, but it is difficult to see how the cause will be advanced by compelling a person to send for a pint when perhaps they may only require half that quantity. The sealing business is a most difficult affair and how people when they are busy will find the time to cork and seal a bottle containing a pint for 4d we fail to see. The Act may also cause a certain amount of inconvenience to parents, but it will undoubtedly benefit the rising generation. In small towns and villages there is probably no harm arising from "Tommy" fetching his father's supper beer, but in the crowed cities the custom leads to all sorts of evil; on the whole the Act will probably be beneficial.

DESTRUCTION OF WALLS

The walls on either side of Crown Lane are certainly being damaged and the stones thrown on the path causing obstruction. It seems rather strange that mischievous people who seem to delight in this kind of thing cannot be detected and brought to justice.

FISH AND CHIPS

We have asked if the itinerant vendors of fried fish and other savoury edibles who traverse the streets of Witney pay any rates or tolls. We think they do not, although we believe they are liable to the latter.

FAT STOCK SHOW

The fat stock show at Witney on the 20th was a very successful one. This was especially the case as far as quality was concerned. The beef was particularly good and realised high prices. The dinner in the evening too was a capital social function under the genial chairmanship of the senior Bailiff, Mr W. Smith J. P.

Menu

Cod fish, Oyster sauce

Filleted Plaice.

Roast Turkey Roast Chicken

Tongue.

Sirloin Beef Boiled Mutton

Pheasant.

Plum Pudding

Mince Pies Tartlets

Jellies Blanc Mange

Custard.

Cheese and Celery.

1902

There was rejoicing everywhere in June, when the Boers capitulated and the War ended at last.

The Coronation celebrations did not turn out quite as expected: the unfortunate Edward VII developed acute appendicitis, and had to have an operation two days before the planned date of June 26. Postponement was inevitable. The King wished festivities to proceed as planned, and in London, on July 6, no fewer than 456,000 poor people were entertained to dinner in public halls all over the capital. In Witney, however, it was not too difficult to re-schedule the celebrations for the new date of August 9.

In Westminster, Mr Balfour succeeded Lord Salisbury as Prime Minister. The campaign for votes for women was supported by a 37,000-signature petition presented to Parliament by women textile workers; the Gazette does not mention whether Witney operatives were involved in any way.

The Education Bill aroused much argument. Should there be religious education in schools, and if so, which religion, and who should pay for it? Witney, with its strong Nonconformist connections, was heavily involved in the controversy.

In August the Imperial Vaccination League was formed. The smallpox epidemic was causing serious concern both nationally and locally, though Witney itself seems to have been spared. An isolation hospital was set up at Shipton Barrow to provide very basic care for sufferers from infectious diseases.

THE RECTOR'S GOLDEN WEDDING

Monday December 30th was the Golden Wedding anniversary of the Rector and Mrs Foxley Norris. The couple received many good wishes and gifts, including a framed address in gold lettering signed by every member of the choir. In the afternoon a peal of 5,040 changes was rung on the bells of St. Mary's Church in 3 hours 2 minutes. On the next evening, at the Witney Ringers' supper, the Rector and Mrs Foxley Norris received a surprise gift of a dinner gong consisting of eight sweetly sounding bells tuned in distonic scale. After speeches of thanks, toasts and songs, the New Year was rung in by all the bells of St. Mary's.

DISTINGUISHED VISITORS IN WITNEY

The Duke of Marlborough and his cousin, Mr Winston Churchill M.P, came to Witney to enrol recruits for the Queen's Own Hussars Imperial Yeomanry, and also to visit the recently opened Witney Institute, where they agreed to play a game of billiards. Mr Churchill won. His Grace expressed great interest in the club, and said he intended to present it with a second billiard table. Mr Churchill also spoke in praise of the Institute, commending its policy of being non-party, non-sectarian, non-class and non-alcoholic.

His Grace has recently been promoted to Major in the Yeomanry, and Mr Churchill has been appointed Captain to fill the vacancy thus created.

SWINE FEVER RULES BREACHED

Mark Fifield, gardener at the Witney Union Workhouse, was summoned for moving a pig without having a licence to do so, at Witney, on the 6th inst. PC Hancox stated that he saw the defendant driving a pig in Corn Street. Defendant said he did not know a licence was required. The pig was then taken back to the Workhouse. Fine 7s 6d.

WORKHOUSE CHRISTMAS TREE

On Friday January 3rd the inmates of the Witney Union Workhouse had their annual Christmas Tree. Donated by Mr Mason of Eynsham Hall, the huge tree was laden with pipes and tobacco for the old men, cakes and useful articles for the women, and toys, workboxes and writing cases for the children. An evening of vocal and instrumental music was enjoyed in the tastefully decorated hall.

HUNTING ACCIDENTS

Four persons were injured during a run with the East Berks hounds on Jan 11th. Frightened by two galloping hunters, the horse drawing Mr and Mrs Douglas's trap bolted, and collided with Miss Batt's horse. She was slightly injured, and Mr Douglas was thrown from the trap. Mrs Douglas, alone behind the bolting horse, soon fell from the vehicle, fracturing her skull. Mr Ripley caught the horse but a blow from the shaft brought him and his mount to the ground. In separate accidents, Mr Holton was thrown, injuring his foot, and a lady driving a trap escaped unhurt when it shed a wheel.

RSPCA ANIMAL NEGLECT CASES

A farmer and his labourer were fined £3 and 10s respectively for neglecting two horses. Another farmer was fined £1 for the same offence, but the case against a third was dismissed.

PING PONG TOURNAMENT

The new indoor game proved popular with spectators and players at the Ping Pong Tournament held at the Corn Exchange over two days. There were 60 entries and two divisions. Miss Smith beat Miss Cheatle in the ladies' final, and the gentlemen's champion was Mr Mavrogordato, a Greek citizen who beat a fellow-student at Oxford, Mr Vernon Harcourt.

HIS GRACE'S GIFT

The Witney Institute has received the oak billiard table promised by the Duke of Marlborough, and the billiard room has been enlarged to measure 45ft by 20ft. The committee has decided to furnish a room for Ping Pong, and is planning to set up tennis and Fives courts in the field. Membership is now over 200.

POSTMAN WIGGINS PETITION

Shocked at the news that Postman John Wiggins is to retire because of age without being entitled to a pension, the principal inhabitants of the town have signed a petition in the hope of obtaining substantial recognition of the impeccable 30-year record of this much-respected public servant.

SKATING

By kind permission of J. Mason Esq., hundreds of people enjoyed skating on Eynsham Hall Lake in early February. Large parties from Oxford also skated on Blenheim Lake.

DEATH OF A YEOMAN

Mr J. W. Harris, aged 23, whose father lives in Hailey, has died of enteric fever while fighting for his country as an Imperial Yeoman in South Africa.

SMALLPOX EPIDEMIC

The smallpox epidemic in London is causing many who oppose the vaccination regulations on conscientious grounds to think again. Statistics show that this remedy really works against the disease, which has plagued the world for so long, and the risk of infection is dangerously close now.

*

26

PRESENTATION TO POSTMAN

On his retirement, Postman Wiggins was presented with an umbrella and walking stick, both silver mounted, and a pair of gold spectacles by the staff of the Witney Post Office.

WORKHOUSE ASSAULT CASE

A 16-year-old boy, an inmate of the Workhouse, was sentenced to one month's imprisonment for assaulting the porter and kicking a nurse in the chest. The boy had previously lived at the Workhouse, but had come under Dr. Barnardo's care, and that gentleman sent him out to Canada. He was, however, sent back, and Dr. Barnardo had returned him to the Guardians on the day the assault was committed.

STREET OBSTRUCTIONS

Shopkeepers and ratepayers are protesting about the ice-cream vendors from outside Witney who are waiting outside all the schools, obstructing the streets and catching every half-penny the children have to spend. They pay no rates, unlike the local shopkeepers whose custom they are taking.

EDUCATION BILL

Under the new Education Bill the School Boards are to be abolished: County Councils will become in effect the new School Boards. This means that women are to be excluded in the educational oversight of children. They were eligible to be members of School Boards, but not of County or Borough Councils. As half the children are girls, women's participation does seem necessary. Under the Bill Nonconformists will be at liberty to build and support their own new schools at their own expense.

POSTMAN WIGGINS

In spite of the petition sent on his behalf, the Post Office has declined to award Mr Wiggins any kind of pension or allowance whatever.

THEATRICAL TRIUMPH

Two comedies, 'Mrs Hilary Regrets' and 'Meg's Diversion', played to a packed Corn Exchange. Many local amateurs gave of their best, and more similar evenings are looked forward to.

THEFT OF CLOTHES

A tramp pleaded guilty to stealing two suits of boys' clothes, value 12s 6d, from Valentine and Barrell's shop. He said he had stolen the goods and tried to sell them because he was hungry, but later took them to the Police Station and asked to be arrested. He was sentenced to 14 days' hard labour.

NEW BELL ROPE

The Council agreed to purchase a new bell rope for the Cemetery Chapel, costing 7s or 8s.

TRAIN SERVICE

After much high-level discussion, the 'improved' train service consists of only one extra train from and to Oxford in the afternoon. A full revision of the timetable had been hoped for, with an earlier down train so that Witney residents might get their newspapers before 10am.

ISOLATION HOSPITAL

The Council has decided to take the property offered by Mr Maddox for use as an isolation hospital. It consists of a cottage with stable and large barn, at Shipton Barrow. A retaining fee of £20 a year would be payable, with £40 extra if the place is used for smallpox cases.

VOLUNTEER DANCE

F Company Oxfordshire Light Infantry gave a successful dance in the Corn Exchange. Nearly 100 people danced to a volunteer string band until the early hours.

* * * * * * * * * * * * * * * * *

CORONATION PLANS

The Bailiffs' plans for the town's celebrations on June 26th and 27th include a procession; dinner for 1000 men; tea for 1000 women and 1000 children; sports; a bonfire and fireworks. A 4d rate would raise £210 to cover expenses. The Council approves.

WORKHOUSE FARE

The Witney Board of Guardians has decided to allow Workhouse inmates extra fare on the first Coronation Day.

EARLY ECLIPSE?

On May 7th a strange phenomenon was observed: darkness started to fall at 4pm, and street lighting had to be turned on. At a Bampton cricket match, players lost sight of the ball. A solar eclipse had been forecast for midnight, but it is not known if this was the reason for the occurrence.

CORONATION COMPLICATIONS

The Bailiffs handed over the organisation of the Coronation celebrations to the Council, as the latter wished to control the spending of the proposed 4d rate rather than allowing the Bailiffs to do so. They refused to meet a Council deputation, as their minds were made up. The large Committee was dissolved, and a new one formed. The idea of a 4d rate was abandoned in favour of voluntary subscriptions, which would be fairer to those with little money. The new Committee decided to provide free dinners to persons over 60, tea for children, fireworks and a bonfire. The Oddfellows would carry out the ox roast.

EGG THIEVES

Two boys, aged 12 and 11, were ordered to receive 6 and 4 stripes of the birch respectively for stealing 10 duck eggs, value 5s, from Mr Shuffrey's farm.

AGRICULTURAL SHOW

Each prominent local town holds the Oxfordshire Agricultural Society Show once in ten years. This year it was Witney's turn. The town was decorated with flags and bunting, and illuminations at night. Horses, sheep and cattle were shown over the two days. Among local businesses displaying their wares were: Leigh & Son and Long & Son (agricultural machinery), Hollis & Son (carts and wagons), T. W. Cook (carts), Looker (traps), Ford (rope etc), the Witney Blanket Company. A luncheon was held in a huge marquee, and the Band of the Grenadier Guards played. Mr Eaton the Stationmaster, Messrs Payne & Son the Carriers and Supt Hawtin of the Police dealt efficiently with the large crowds attending. A few cases of drunkenness and theft occurred.

PEACE AT LAST

On June 1st the happy news was received that the war in South Africa was over. Englishmen and women everywhere are rejoicing at the conclusion of this cruel conflict. Witney celebrated with street decorations, a Thanksgiving Service with merry peals on the bells, a torchlight procession with the town band, and fireworks followed by the singing of the National Anthem and Rule Britannia. The Bailiffs held a large dinner at the Corn Exchange with loyal toasts, songs, music and speeches. Among those present were several men who had fought in the war.

MARKET PROBLEM

Witney Market is in danger of being closed by the Board of Agriculture unless it can be held in a properly paved and drained area approved by the Board for the sale of cattle, sheep and pigs. The lower portion of Church Green has been suggested.

BISHOP'S VISIT

The Bishop of Oxford arrived by train to make several visits in Witney. He braved the steep staircase at Saint Mary's to greet the bellringers in their chamber.

KING'S ILLNESS SHOCK

On June 24th it was announced that His Majesty had been operated on for appendicitis. Though he had expressed a wish for the coronation celebrations to proceed as planned, the Witney Committee decided to postpone

them indefinitely. Fortunately the oxen bought for the occasion had not been killed, and the cake was sold off cheaply. Intercessory services were held at Saint Mary's and the Wesleyan Church.

COMING OF AGE

Some 400 persons travelled to Weymouth to celebrate the coming-of-age of Mr J. H. Early, of Messrs C. Early & Co. Fine weather, a stroll on the parade, an excellent dinner and a boat trip to Portland to visit the Verne Citadel, the convict prison, the Chesil Beach and the training ship "Minotaur" all made the trip most enjoyable. At dinner there were toasts and speeches, and the young man received several substantial gifts from the staff.

NO SMALLPOX HERE

The recent rumour of a smallpox case in Witney is entirely without foundation. The town is quite free from any kind of contagious disease. There are, however, several cases at Bampton.

ISOLATION HOSPITAL

The Isolation Hospital is proving satisfactory for the treatment of the Bampton smallpox victims, though a bathroom and accommodation for nurses and helpers should be provided in the barn. Tents may be purchased to hold more patients. Unfortunately the remoteness of the building has caused delay and confusion in transporting sufferers.

G.F.S. OUTING

Members of the Witney Girls' Friendly Society enjoyed their summer outing. After the festival service at Broadwell Church, they proceeded to Kencot Manor, where they were entertained by a band playing on the lawn. Mr Milward, of Langford, kindly brought over his gramophone, which caused much amusement.

WITNEY MAN REMOVED THE KING

His Majesty is now well enough to spend part of his convalescence on the Royal Yacht at Portsmouth. He was removed from the Palace to Victoria Station in one of Messrs Reading's invalid carriages; this company is led by Mr W.J. Shuffrey of Witney. The carriage was re-upholstered for the occasion, and provided with curtains to ensure the royal patient's privacy.

TEACHERS' VISIT

About 60 National Union of Teachers members from the Oxford & District branch spent a pleasant day in Witney by invitation of their President, Mr J.C. Sims. After visiting Witney

Mills they lunched at the Temperance Hotel, then went to Saint Mary's Church and the Priory. After tea, taken in the Recreation Ground, Mr J. V. Early addressed the visitors on the importance of a teacher's life.

CHURCH SCHOOLS TREAT

The children of Saint Mary's, Holy Trinity and Curbridge schools marched through the streets carrying beautiful garlands and headed by Bridge Street Mills Band. On their way to Saint Mary's the boys performed a flag drill. Tea followed the short service, and in the evening there were sports and a firework display. Mr Merrick, who has just finished his apprenticeship at Saint Mary's, was presented with a Gladstone bag.

CORONATION DATE
The Coronation will take place on August 9th

MEDICAL COMMENTS

The Medical Officer in charge of the Isolation Hospital reports that the recent epidemic is almost completely over, and in any case was mild and limited, thanks to vaccination. However, another doctor, who wishes to remain anonymous, warns of the dangers of failing to notify cases of scarlatina and diphtheria. If children with these diseases are not treated correctly, and are allowed to mix with others, serious epidemics may occur. Also, drinking water supplies should be checked regularly, and a less casual attitude to infection adopted.

CORONATION CELEBRATIONS

With the exception of refreshment houses all the business establishments were closed, and the day was entirely devoted to pleasure.

OX ROASTS

Very early in the morning the Oddfellows started roasting an ox on a brick fireplace opposite the Corn Exchange. Some 70 persons enjoyed the roast beef at a midday dinner in the Upper Room of the Corn Exchange. Others bought plates of beef to take home. Another ox roast was held in Corn Street, near 'Parliament House'.

SPORTS

As well as Flat Races, the children competed keenly in novelty events such as Flag Gathering, Bicycle and Three-legged races (boys) and Egg and Spoon and Skipping (girls).

CHILDREN'S EVENTS

At 2.30 nearly 1500 youngsters assembled at Woodgreen. They marched to The Leys with flags, banners and music provided by Bridge Street Mills Band and the Wesleyan Band of Hope Drum and Fife Band. After tea on The Leys the younger children were presented with Coronation mugs and the older ones with cups and saucers.

TORCHLIGHT PROCESSION AND FIREWORKS

Some 5000 people watched the first firework display, which started after the torchlight procession had marched from West End to The Leys. Then a huge bonfire was lit, and a second display started at 10.15. Numerous decorations and illuminations on business premises gave the town a very festive air.

OLD PEOPLE'S DINNER

At 12.30 about 200 people over 60 sat down to roast and boiled beef, pork, ham, veal, vegetables and plum pudding. An ounce of tobacco was given to each man. The Rector proposed a loyal toast, which was received with cheers for the King and Queen. Catering was by Mrs Hadley of the Marlborough Hotel.

OX ROAST IN CORN STREET

DUCK SHOOT

Mr Mason of Eynsham Hall has recovered from his recent illness, and was able to attend the successful duck shoot held on his estate.

OX ROAST MONEY FOR CHARITY

The balance left from the Corn Street Coronation ox-roast, £9 0s 9d, has been forwarded to the Oxford Infirmary.

REV. BYLES LEAVES

The Wesleyan Minister, Rev. G. V. Byles, completed his three years in the Witney circuit. At a farewell service he preached his final sermon. The new minister, Rev T. Hardy Banks BA, is taking over immediately.

CHILD ASSAULT CASE

At Petty Sessions a labourer was accused of assaulting a girl aged seven. It was alleged that he committed the offence in the stable of the Holly Bush public house, afterwards giving her a penny. He was committed for trial at the next Quarter Sessions.

WHITHER WITNEY MARKET?

The Council has a difficult decision to make in view of the Board of Agriculture's order that the Market must be moved, or at least made more hygienic. A new market would probably cost £1000, while tarmacadaming the existing Market Place would cost £230. Arguments are heated, and there is also a problem with the Duke of Marlborough, who has not been co-operative. He is willing to extend the lease on the Market Place in the event of its being improved, but will not hear of any interference with his manorial rights.

KING OF CRICKET AT WITNEY

The great Dr. W. G. Grace has honoured Witney with his presence, visiting Witney Feast and playing for the town against the Hon. R. Hardinge's XI. He delighted the large crowd with his affability and excellent style, scoring 25 runs and bowling with his usual brilliance. Another cricketing hero, G. L. Jessop, also played superbly. The score was Witney: 245, the Hon R. Hardinge's XI: 54.

WITNEY FEAST

This year the attractions pitched on Church Green were arranged to face the roadway to avoid disturbing traffic to the station. Mr Alf Ball's cinematograph was the best show of all, with clear slides of local workers leaving the factories, an accident on the bridge, and a drama entitled The Soldier's Return. We are glad to see that freak shows, with their fat ladies, skeletons etc, have quite gone out of favour.

ISOLATION HOSPITAL STAYS

It was agreed that the Isolation Hospital should continue for another year, at a cost of £25 rent and 14s a week for the Caretaker.

W. G. GRACE BATS FOR WITNEY

33

EDUCATION BILL

The Education Bill is arousing much opposition, mainly because it is seen as depriving Nonconformist children of their right to be educated according to their own religion. Only Anglican schools would be funded by public money: Nonconformists were expected to finance their own schools.

CASE DISMISSED

At Quarter Sessions, the labourer indicted for assaulting a 7-year-old girl at Witney was found not guilty and discharged.

NEW WORKHOUSE MASTER AND MATRON

Mr and Mrs T.J. Finnis have been selected from over 300 applicants to take over control of Witney Workhouse. They are at present in charge of the Petworth, West Sussex, Workhouse, and will move to Witney in November.

THE TRAMP NUISANCE

In Witney this month four men, all tramps, were sentenced to 14 days in prison, one for being drunk and the others for begging. A French tramp was sent to prison for three weeks for stealing a coat, and a woman received a three months' sentence for drunkenness and breaking two windows, one being that of the cell at the Police Station.

MARRIAGE OF FAMOUS CRICKETER

Mr Gilbert Jessop married Miss Millicent Osborne, of New South Wales, in London. The couple met during the recent visit of the English cricket team to Australia. Mr Jessop's finest performance so far was at the Oval in August, when he scored 104. He played in a special match at Witney in September, also honoured by the presence of the great Dr W.G. Grace.

HUGE PUMPKINS

Mr Taylor, gardener of Cokethorpe Park, has grown pumpkins weighing 54, 55, 64 and 71 pounds.

FIRE BRIGADE COMPETITION

Saint Mary's Close, Witney, was the location for the second annual Fire Brigade Competition. Events included One Man Drill, Four Man Drill, Six Man Drill (wet drill), Ladder and Bucket Race, Hose Race and Tug of War. Witney overpowered its rivals to win the Cup, kindly donated by Mr Oates, and presented by Miss Mason of Eynsham Hall. A most enjoyable Smoking Concert was then held at the Corn Exchange.

NEW BAILIFFS

Mr W. Hitchman and Mr L. Druce were elected at the annual Court of His Grace the Duke of Marlborough, held at the Town Hall. They later withdrew, explaining that they had not been asked whether they were willing to stand, and that others in the hall might have wished to be considered. However, they finally decided to accept, to the relief of some who feared that the town would be left without Bailiffs to administer, among other things, the Bread and Beef Charity which provided generously for poor people at Christmas. If the Charity Commissioners had to be called in, who knew what unpleasant decisions they might make.

RECORD SCHOOL ATTENDANCE

At Saint Mary's Boys' School, a full attendance of 121 pupils, both morning and afternoon, was recorded in one week.

BELLS FOR THE KING

His Majesty's birthday was celebrated by the Witney Ringing Society with peals of bells in the tower of Saint Mary's Church.

POSTMAN'S THANKS

John Wiggins begs to return his sincere thanks to the inhabitants of Witney and neighbourhood, for their great kindness in presenting him with a sum of money on his retirement from the duties of postman.

DRAINAGE SYSTEM DRAMA

The cost of the Drainage Scheme, which was to have been £7000, has risen to over £16,000. At an inquiry conducted by Major Stewart, Inspector from the Local Government Board, many searching questions were asked about the problems, both technical and financial, encountered by the Council. The whole project has proved much more complicated than had been expected, and much criticism is being levelled at the Council .

COUNCIL PLEADS POVERTY

The Council has written to Major Stewart, Inspector from the Local Government Board, applying for an additional sewage loan of £1437 3s 7d, and stating that the Council has no money in hand to meet its £375 debt to the contractors. Lack of money is causing the work to be delayed.

WITNEY SCHOOL OF SCIENCE AND ART

After an exhibition of the students' work in the Wesleyan School, the annual prize-giving was held in the Lecture Theatre of the Technical Schools. Science subjects studied last year were Maths, Chemistry (theoretical and practical) and Physiography. In Art, students learned Freehand, Light and Shade, Model, Perspective, Geometry, Painting in Sepia, Water-colours and Oils from casts, copies and from nature. Sir William Markby (after distributing the prizes) praised Mr Sims for his organisation of the evening classes, but as Chairman of the County Council Finance Committee he could not hold out any hope of greater financial help in the future. Could generous Witney persons perhaps assist in the matter?

BIRCH FOR DELINQUENT

A boy of thirteen was sentenced to twelve stripes of the birch for stealing a sovereign from his employer's wife's purse. His previous offences include stealing eggs and forging a letter under his employer's name .

WITNEY GRAMMAR AND TECHNICAL SCHOOL

At the first prize-giving under the new amalgamated scheme, Mr Haines, the Principal, reported that the experiment of teaching girls and boys in the same classes was so far an unqualified success. There were twelve girls on the register. Total pupil numbers were: First Term 36, Second Term 35, Third Term 43.

SWINDLERS AT WORK

Readers are again warned about worthless Directories, and a new swindle in which some local people sent half a guinea to the 'Trafalgar Novelty Co' for a practically worthless pen, under the promise that they could earn £1 a week by writing ten letters a day. The swindler has been arrested.

1903

The government was considering a new law to introduce the registration and numbering of private cars. Local speed limits would be determined by County Councils, and speeding fines were increased. These measures were not nearly severe enough to satisfy 'Jottings', who never lost his loathing of the motor car with its noise, dust, and danger to pedestrians and horses.

Public services were very much in the news. The water tower was finished at last, though its appearance was not much admired. Pipe-laying and drainage work was still proceeding, but there was serious disagreement over connection to the sewage system. Why should people with perfectly good earth closets have to go to the expense of getting connected?

Gas mains were being installed in parts of Witney, causing more road works to annoy residents. In July the Gasworks itself gave its neighbours a nasty shock.

One case of smallpox was reported in the town centre, but the medical authorities took prompt and strict hygienic measures, and the infection did not spread.

THE COUNCIL DOES A GOOD JOB

The frost ended with what is called a silver thaw. On Saturday the rain, which fell on frozen ground, formed a solid sheet of ice, which made travelling exceedingly difficult and dangerous. In numerous instances horses had to be taken out of the conveyances they were drawing, and the latter left on the side of the road. Happily the thaw came the next day. We congratulate the U.D.C. on the prompt manner in which the dangerous state of the footways was dealt with. In less than an hour the pavement was well sprinkled with gravel, and doubtless many accidents were thus avoided.

DRINK DRIVING

It cannot be said that the Witney justices erred on the side of severity in fining a horse dealer only 15/- for being drunk in charge of a horse and trap. This offence is far more serious than an ordinary case of drunkenness, for whereas in the latter case it is only the drunkard himself as a rule who runs the risk, the drunk driver of a conveyance is a source of danger to all users of the King's highway, and he should be made to feel this in no unmistakable way when he commits the offence.

William Austin pleaded guilty to being drunk in charge of a horse and cart. P.C. Purdy said that the defendant was coming up Witney High Street with a horse and cart on the night of 23rd January. He had no lights and was drunk. He was taken into custody and released the next morning. The defendant was not driving the horse. He had no control over the horse. Supt. Hawtin said he had been told that the defendant on the same day had caused an accident in Bridge Street.
Fined 15/-.

AN OLD CUSTOM DIES

It is now some four and thirty years ago that the celebrated Mr Horsley, curate of Witney, instituted the Witney twelfth night party. The annual fixture has been carried out with more or less success ever since. The committee have decided to abandon it. The reason is that the entertainment does not pay its way, but each year leaves the committee further in debt.

Well, it is an old saying that "Nothing lasts long in Witney"

PIG KEEPERS' CLUB SUPPER

The members of the Witney Working Men's Pig Club had a supper at the Three Horse Shoes public house in Corn Street. Twenty people sat down to a

Corn Street Stores Christmas display

fine meal presided over by Mr. A.. E. Horne the Secretary. The repast, which was done full justice to, was placed on the table by Host Moss-Holland.

FEWER TRAMPS

During the past nine weeks 327 tramps have been received at the Witney Union Workhouse against 538 for the corresponding period last year.

BREAD AND BEEF CHARITY

On Christmas Eve bread and beef was distributed to the poor of the town by the Bailiffs (Messrs W. Hitchman and L. Druce). 26 cwt of beef was distributed among 595 families or 2398 persons, 7 cwt of loaves were given away, and 101 widows received 4d each.

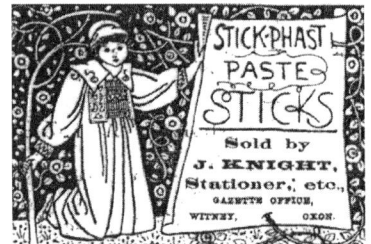

ALIENS IN ENGLAND

The admittance of alien paupers into England is a question that will have to be grappled with sooner or later. Why our shores should become the asylum for undesirables from other nations we cannot conceive. Of late years this evil has been growing at an alarming rate and if something is not done England will soon be over-run with foreigners of the worst class. At the present time foreign competition in the labour market is being severely felt in London and other large centres. The skilled English Mechanic is gradually being ousted by the alien who will work cheaply and lives hard. Such a state of things cannot be allowed to continue. A measure which had as its object the restriction of immigration would be welcome by all who live in this crowded little island.

POLLUTED WATER

Mr M. Florey drew the attention of the Council to the condition of the stream that flowed through Standlake. At times the water was like soap suds. There are several houses in the village that have no other water supply. Mr Holtom said it no doubt came from a mill at Witney. It was sometimes so bad in Ducklington that his horse would not drink. He also remarked that it did not come from the Cogges stream as the stream at Gill Mill was clear. The matter was referred to the Thames Conservancy.

THE KING IS UNWELL

The King's health is again giving cause for anxiety to his subjects. His Majesty's intended visit to Chatsworth has been abandoned and it is stated that he is suffering from a bout of influenza. The King is at present confined to his room.

WATER PIPELINE NEARLY COMPLETE

Messrs Rowell & Son the contractors who are carrying out the water supply scheme at Witney are getting on remarkably well with their work, Bridge Street, West End, Woodgreen, Church Green, Station Road and the Union Hill pipes have been laid down. We understand the scheme is being carried out in a thoroughly workmanlike manner and it is rumoured that the expenditure will not exceed the contract price.

THE STATE OF OUR ROADS

Dear Sir,
 It has long puzzled me why some of the roads are partially metalled, if so strong a term can be appropriately used with stone that you can cut with a knife however blunt that knife may be. I will not specify these roads, but I will exempt the Witney – Burford Highway. Let me ask anyone to watch the effects of a heavily-laden wagon passing over a newly laid patch of rubble: every bit crumbles to dust forthwith, and melts to mud at the next shower. This may be amusing to some but to me it is amazing.

Yours faithfully,
Scrutator

PAVING THE SQUARE

It has been resolved by the U.D.C. to pave a certain portion of Market Square at a cost of £180. Why should the ratepayer pay for the paving of the market that does not belong to them? The Lord of the Manor, the Duke of Marlborough, claims that it is his property. If it is let him pay for the paving of the square, or if he will not, let the Council take the market to another site.

THE SCRUTATOR Would like to know:

How many people have got wet feet by stepping into a pool of water close to the bridge at the end of Crown Lane?

Whether the town surveyor or his deputy could spend a few minutes occasionally to inspect the footpaths?

If the U.D.C. thinks it is safe to have no barrier to prevent horses and cattle straying out of Langle and up Crown Lane to the great peril of pedestrians?

Who is the owner of the terrier in Newland who habitually flies at cyclists and pedestrians?

Whether the owner knows the risk he is running keeping such an animal?

CHANGE IN OPENING TIMES

The County Licensing Committee has declared all areas with a population of less than 1000 inhabitants not to be populous places. The result of this is that all public houses in villages must close at 9 o'clock on Sunday evenings and 10 o'clock on other days of the week.

It is probable that the changes will be for the good in most places, 10 o'clock being late enough for people to get their supper beer, or the extra pint to digest the supper. In some places the law may cause not a little inconvenience. Let us imagine that an inhabitant of Aston or Cote arrives at Bampton station by the last train at night, by the time he has walked the mile and a half into Bampton he may require, let us say, a drop of lemonade or something more stimulating. He must trudge along for another 2 miles, his thirst unquenched. Still on the whole the new arrangement may work all right and in time the public will get accustomed to the change, as they did with the 11 o'clock closing some 30 years ago. There is one exception made in this matter with regard to the parish of Cogges. That part of Newland as far as the spot where the old toll gate used to stand is, for the purposes of the Licensing Act, to be deemed to be part of the town of Witney.

♦♦♦♦♦♦♦♦♦♦♦♦♦♦

SMALLPOX

A tramp staying in the common lodging house in Corn Street was discovered to be suffering from smallpox. He has been removed to the isolation hospital at Wychwood. The lodging house has been closed, the inmates isolated, and no further cases have occurred.

GETTING CONNECTED

Will the council be insisting that every house is connected to the new sewer? The drainage of the town has proved a very expensive affair and has inflicted a burden upon the rate payers which will be well nigh intolerable for the next quarter of a century. This will be felt more acutely by the owners of small properties than by any other class in the community, many of them at the present time hardly know how to find the money to pay the rates. We repeat that the new sewage system was brought about in order to comply with the demands of the Thames Conservancy with regard to the pollution of Emm's Ditch, and there is no reason whatever why people whose premises are in a sanitary condition should be compelled to bear the cost of connection to a system so imperfect in its conception, and which is open to criticism from a health point of view.

URBAN DISTRICT COUNCIL ELECTIONS

Nine people have been nominated to fill the 4 vacant seats on the U.D.C. They are:

Harry Robins, West End.
John Knight, 20 High Street, Stationer.
Caleb Viner, 32 Bridge Street, Grocer and Draper.
William Smith, Windrush House, Manufacturer.
Isaac Solomon Dingle, 38 High Street, Boot Maker.
Frederick Middleton, 68 Mill Street, Factory Foreman.
Samuel Shuffrey, 7 Woodgreen, Farmer.
Albert Edward Horne, 150 Corn Street, Corn merchant.
Albert Leopold Napoleon Long, 89 Corn Street, Builder

SMALLPOX FREE
LODGING HOUSE CONDEMNED

The town is now free of any suspected cases of the disease. The inmates of the lodging house in Corn Street, who have been under observation for 20 days, have now been discharged. The whole of the clothing, bedding etc belonging to the proprietors and lodgers have been burned, and the premises have been thoroughly disinfected. Dr Cole, the Medical Officer of Health, has certified the house to be unfit for a common lodging house and it will therefore cease to be used for that purpose.

During the past 20 days the inmates of the house were kept supplied with food, plenty of beer and various games.

To the Ratepayers of Witney:

At a meeting held in Corn Street on Wednesday 18th inst, it was decided to elect two candidates to represent Corn Street on the Urban District Council. We the undersigned were chosen for nomination and should you do us the honour to elect us, we will do our best to keep down the rates. We do not bind ourselves to any one policy, except to go against the compulsory connection to the sewers.

Where there are earth closets and a good supply of water, we believe that should be sufficient to satisfy the demands of the Local Government Board.

We are yours respectfully,
Albert L. N. Long
Albert E. Horne.

DEATH OF MR MASON

Mr. J. Mason died at Eynsham Hall at 4.30 in the morning of April 2nd.

The late Mr. Mason came to Eynsham Hall in 1867. The estate formerly belonged to the Earl of Macclesfield. When the estate came into the deceased gentleman's possession he at once set to work to improve it. He made the beautiful lake, extended the park and planted trees extensively. He carried out the improvements with the thoroughness with which he did everything.

He was a Magistrate, and became an ex-officio Guardian of the Witney Union Workhouse. For some years he was an officer of the Yeomanry, and in 1869 he was High Sheriff of the county. He was not merely a member of the Royal Agricultural Society but a practical member. He was continually making experiments and contributed to the discovery of the fixation of nitrogen by leguminous plants. He was well known in the mining world. It was due to his energy and exceptional knowledge of chemistry, that the San Domingas mine became so successful.

In the benevolent world Mr Mason was well known. The Radcliffe Infirmary is indebted for many thousands of pounds, also the Eye Hospital and the Sarah Acland Home.

He was a brilliant conversationalist and possessed a rich musical voice.

GREAT CANADIAN BOOM

INTENDING EMIGRANTS will do well to book by Allen Line of Royal Mail Steamers for Canada. Also for America by that splendid fleet the White Star, including *Cedric,* the largest vessel ever built. Lowest possible rates consistent with comfort, speed and safety.

Sole Agent for Witney:-
H. T. TITCOMB, saddler, Corn St, from whom all information can be obtained.

ASPHALTING THE SQUARE

The U.D.C. have resolved not withstanding objections to spend some £180 on asphalting Witney Market Square.

It is doubtful if ever such a golden opportunity of taking the market out of the streets will occur again. As this paper argued months ago, if the market must be held in the town, the ideal place is the lower portion of Church Green which could easily be asphalted up to the first gravel path or further if required. The advantages of the Green over the present site are numerous and obvious. In the first place the unpleasant smell would be removed further from the houses, and we do not see why the traders living in the Market Square, some of whom we know would be glad to have the market removed, should be compelled to have this nuisance right under their noses. Another advantage is the sheep and pigs could be penned together, whereas at present they are all over the place. Then on the Green there would be no traffic whereas in Market Square there will be a constant danger of horses slipping up as well as pedestrians.

The Green is the playground for children, and if part of it were asphalted there would be a dry place for them in the winter, which would save damage done to the Green proper by trampling on it in wet weather.

A more important matter still is that of the fair. The heavy traffic that so spoils the grass might be put on the paved area. Is it too late for the Council to change its mind?

******

DRINKING WATER FOR ALL

In council Mr Early moved that on and after 31 August the Council should discontinue the supply of drinking water by cart and the collection of night soil round the town. The sewage system and water supply was up and working. Why should the Council continue supplying drinking water? The Council agreed, but night soil collection to continue.

THE STREETS ARE UP AGAIN

The Witney Gas Company is now laying new mains in the lower part of the town; this is necessary, we understand, due to the increased demand for gas, especially at the Witney Mills. Eight-inch mains are being laid from the gas works into the street and thence six-inch mains to the bridge and four-inch to Witney Mill. This will give a better supply to the lower half of the town.

SALE OF HOUSES IN THE CROFTS

The following houses in the Crofts were sold by auction.

Nos. 58 & 60 purchased by H. Moss £230.

Nos. 62 & 64 purchased by H.T. Ravenor £220.

Nos. 66 & 68 purchased by W.F. Harwood £225.

Nos. 70 & 72 purchased by John Williams £230.

Nos. 74, 76 &78 purchased by John Williams £360.

BUSINESS EXPANSION

Considerable alterations have been made to the business premises of Messrs Henry Long & Son in the High Street. The shop has been extended and the workshop accommodation largely increased. The whole house is now used for business purposes, the upstairs rooms being utilised as showrooms for sanitary appliances, and other things connected with the trade.

WET WET WET

The rain fell for over sixty hours and over four inches of rain fell. The lamentable sight of floods in June on all the low-lying land can be seen everywhere. The road to Ducklington just beyond Emm's Ditch bridge is flooded, as also is the road opposite the park in Ducklington.

Seagulls as far inland as Oxfordshire in the middle of summer is probably a sight never before seen. The birds had evidently lost their bearings and were seen for some hours flying round the flooded fields near Chimney under the impression that it was the open sea.

THE LEYS SHOULD NOT BE BUILT ON

The Leys is on the market for a very reasonable price on the condition that it is never built on. Now is the time for some gentleman to come forward and purchase it as a recreation ground for the town. The auctioneers say that such an opportunity may never occur again.

THE CROFTS AND CAPE TERRACE ROADS

The Roads Committee considered it would be desirable that the Crofts and Cape Terrace be taken over by the Council and the road "made", kerbed and channelled. They recommended that the Council should make an offer to the owners of the properties fronting and adjoining these roads to defray three fifths of the cost of this work.

****

****

FREE FARMS!
NO MORE RENT FOR FARMERS!

The CANADIAN FARMERS' DELEGATES are visiting the
COUNTY OF OXFORD.
Notice of Arrangements will appear later

Any person desiring to meet and consult the Delegates with a view to securing information about Canada drawn from their personal experiences as practical and successful agriculturists are invited to send their names and addresses without delay to

Mr. W. T. R. PRESTON, Commissioner of Emigration,
17, Victoria Street, London, S.W
from whom pamphlets and all particulars can be obtained free

BL

WHITSUNTIDE

On Saturday a large number of visitors for Whitsuntide arrived in Witney. In the town itself on the Monday, beyond a cricket match, there was nothing going on, but the lovely weather which prevailed enabled many people to go to the Faringdon sports, Fairford sports or to Woodstock where the Oxfordshire Yeomanry are camped.

COOKING LECTURE

During the week cooking lectures and demonstrations on gas cooking have been given by Miss Edden. The lectures were under the auspices of the Witney Gas Company and Messrs Fletcher Russel & Co. gas stove makers of Warrington. Mr Arthur L. Leigh welcomed the ladies. In the course of his remarks he stated that when Miss Edden was last here there was only one gas stove in Witney and today there are 250, of which

180 are in small households on slot meters. The Company hoped that the demonstrations would lead to the further use of gas.

ISOLATION HOSPITAL

The expense of the joint temporary Isolation Hospital is sufficiently high to make the people living within the boundaries of the Witney U.D.C. and R.D.C. to wish to form their own permanent hospital. The area covered by the two authorities is a large one covering 50 parishes. A hospital situated in this area would be a boon to the inhabitants and in the case of a serious epidemic would be of inestimable value.

The temporary Hospital at present serves the Chipping Norton and the Witney Union and their Rural Districts, an enormous area, which must create considerable inconvenience and even danger to patients from the outlying parishes.

AT THE MERCY OF THE MAN WITH A PICK

The roads are up again

The Manager of the Gas Company gave an undertaking as far as possible, weather permitting, that no portion of trench should be open for more than 36 hours. The weather recently has been all that could be desired, but the ratepayers of Witney know how far this undertaking has been carried out. Are the ratepayers to be handed over to the tender mercies of the man with the pick?

INCREASED SPEED LIMIT

The Government Motor Bill introduced in the House of Lords proposes to abolish the speed limit and to have all cars registered. Also, penalties are to be more severe than before, but there does not seem to be much protection for the public. Every day we have records of what may almost be called motor murders.

LORDS REJECT POOR BILL

The Poor Law Bill has been rejected by the House of Lords. At present no poor law relief can be given unless the person is "destitute". The result being that members of Friendly Societies are considered "not destitute" when illness occurs, as they are receiving sick pay from the club. The Bill rejected by the Lords would have allowed members of Friendly Societies, although receiving sick pay from the club, to also receive outdoor relief from the Union Workhouse.

****

LAZY

William Bishop, a tramp, was brought before the Magistrates charged with refusing to perform his allotted task whilst in the Witney Union Workhouse.

The Defendant pleaded guilty.

Thomas John Finnis master of the Workhouse, stated the defendant was admitted on Monday night. On Tuesday his task was to pick 8lbs of unbeaten oakum; instead of that he picked only 4oz and refused to do any more.

Supt Hawtin said the prisoner had told him he came from London and did not like work and did not intend to work.

The prisoner asserted he had made a start on the work and had come over queer and rested.

The Chairman, summing up, said "You are lazy and a disgrace to your country."

The Magistrates sentenced the prisoner to one month in prison.

THE GAS WORKS LETTING OFF STEAM

Considerable excitement prevailed in the vicinity of the gas works between ten and eleven on Wednesday evening, caused by the blowing of the safety valve of the gas works boiler. The noise of the steam resembled that of a railway train, and many who had gone to bed hastily got up and rushed into the street. Customers at a nearby hostelry beat a hasty retreat leaving their refreshments in their glasses. Indeed it is said with what degree of truth we know not, that one gentleman has not been seen since.

WANTED – several strong labourers for excavating. $4\frac{1}{2}$d per hour. – Apply foreman, Gazette Office, Witney.

COFFEE TAVERN IN THE BLACK

The Coffee Tavern is within a measurable distance of paying a dividend. The place was established 24 years ago and owing to bad management during the first few years got into financial difficulties, with which it has had to contend ever since.

At the A.G.M. the balance sheet showed a profit of £27 for the year.

SERIOUS CHARGE

Gotobed, a labourer, living at Rozer Hill *(Tower Hill)*, was charged with stealing 31 cigars from the Lamb Inn, Crawley on 4th July. He was also charged with assaulting a policeman on the same day. P.C. Jones stated that he arrested the prisoner, and on the way to the station the prisoner tripped him up and escaped. Gotobed was sentenced to 6 weeks hard labour.

GOOD SCHOOL RESULTS

Mr. Walter Harris, the Head of the Witney Grammar and Technical School, reported that the number of pupils had risen to 51 and said that if growth in numbers increased, a new classroom or lecture theatre with laboratory attached would greatly add to the efficiency of the school.

TO LET at Michaelmas, a desirable RESIDENCE No 64 Corn Street containing:
Two Reception Rooms,
Four Bedrooms,
Good Attics,
Bathroom, Kitchen and
convenient Outbuildings, with two large gardens. – Apply to the Occupier.

NEW LOOK SQUARE

At last the work of tar macadamising the Market Square is finished, and no one who has any regard for the appearance of the town could possibly object to the result.

LAY THE DUST

Is it too much to ask the Surveyor of the W.U.D.C. to give the streets a little more water. This has been an exceptionally showery summer and consequently the water carts have not been much required. When, however, it is a dry day we think the roads should be well watered, especially now the dust raising from motors is so frequently to be seen.

MOTOR CARS TO GO FASTER

The Motor Bill has been passed through Parliament with the result that the speed limit is raised from 12 miles to 20 miles an hour. To be reduced to 10 miles in such places as the local authorities deem expedient. The fines for speeding are much heavier, and for a third offence the Justice may commit the offender to prison.

DISASTROUS HARVEST

Last week the harvest commenced in this district but this week the weather has gone back to its disagreeable mood, wet and windy. Harvest operations have been suspended till the weather clears up. On some of the low lying lands it is difficult to see when the corn will be cut, for the ground is so full of water that the horses sink in several inches with every step. As for getting a binder to work it is simply impossible.

WORKHOUSE CONCERT

On Tuesday evening the Witney String Band gave a concert at the Union Workhouse. The efforts of the performers were much appreciated.

Programme

Post horn Gallop Band
A Japanese Polka Band
Song   *In the dark and dreary sky*
Mr A. Seasons
Song *The village blacksmith*
Mr A. Usher
Banjo and Mandolin
Messrs Richardson & Brice
Song *Dreaming*
Mr S. Richardson
Dance *Barn dance* band
Song (parody) *To be there*
Mr A. Seasons
Banjo Solo *Bluebells of Scotland* Mr S. Richardson
Song *A soldier and a man*
Mr A. Usher
Dance *Belle of Baltimore*
Band
Song *It was mine you know*
Mr S. Richardson
March
March of the prisoners Band
Banjo Solo S. Richardson
Song (parody*) Honeysuckle and the bee* Mr A. Seasons
An Indian Ride Band
GOD SAVE THE KING

LESS DAMAGE TO THE GRASS

Witney Feast will be held in the Market Square and the East side of Church Green. This is the same arrangement as last year. Now that the Council has had the bye-laws for Church Green approved by the Local Government Board, they will have more control to prevent the newly restored Green from being damaged by the fair.

H.M.I. REPORT

Witney Grammar and Technical School has received the following satisfactory report. 'A pleasing improvement has been effected in the work of the school. An able French teacher and a science master of much higher calibre have been added to the staff and have produced a marked effect on the subjects they teach.. The French is oral and is really excellent, and the chemistry and physics have taken a much higher tone. Mathematics is much stronger than formally. More apparatus for practical electricity is urgently needed.'

SAFEGUARDING OUR WATER

In order to keep the new water supply operating efficiently the Witney Urban District Council has decided to build a house at the Water Tower. Too much care cannot be taken of our water supply.

LICENCE REFUSED

George Carr of the Star Inn, Witney applied for an hour's extension on August 3rd the occasion being the corporation dinner. The Bench decided not to grant the extension.

Bath chair (with attendant) for hire. Apply J. Wiggins, High Street, Witney.

45

MILITARY MANOEUVRES

Everything is in readiness for the mimic warfare that is to come off in the country lying between Bristol and Aldershot, and Burford and Southampton. The general idea is that an invading force of 20,000 men under the command of Sir Evelyn Wood lands from the Severn, and a force of 25,000 men under the command of General French is to intercept the enemy's march on London.

Early on Friday morning several batteries of the Royal Field Artillery arrived at Witney Station. The officers and men with their horses and guns came by special train, the first batch arriving at 7 o'clock. The fearful storm of the night had told on the men who had ridden through it across country most of the time. When they got to Witney it was seen that they were drenched to the skin. Fortunately Mr Dring of the Temperance Hotel had received orders to supply them with refreshments, which were served out to the men from a coffee stall by the goods station. Some 500 men were catered for. Each man received a pint of coffee and a certain quantity of cake, which was very acceptable after their night's experience. The guns were unloaded in a very smart manner and the men soon got away, proceeding to Burford where the camp was situated. In all there were four special trains.

PHEASANTS IN SHORT SUPPLY

The first of September 1903 will probably be remembered by sportsmen as one of the worst they have ever experienced. Never within the memory of the present generation has there been such a dearth of birds. The reason, of course, is that the heavy rains during the nesting time destroyed the eggs, or if they were hatched, the young birds. Pheasants are very scarce and some large preserves in the neighbourhood will not have their coverts shot this year.

GASLIGHT OR MOONLIGHT

A correspondent seems to sneer at the Lighting Committee for not lighting the lamps on moonlight nights. We think the Committee are to be congratulated on their economy. Why streetlights should be lit on a full moon night when the lamps actually throw a shadow across the street is incomprehensible to ordinary mortals.

IS IT FAIR

To be or not to be, that's the question. Are the Witney fairs to continue in the town or not? The U.D.C. have failed to cope with the difficulty of providing for fairs and shows that come to town without spoiling the Green, which at very considerable expense has been reclaimed from the wretched state in which it had drifted. We do not hesitate to say that the nuisance to the occupiers of the houses in close proximity to the backs of the various shows has been such that no ratepayer should be expected to tolerate. And the plain duty of the U.D.C. is to see that they are not subject to the indescribably filthy scenes enacted close to their front doors.

Is it not time to move the fairs out of the town and spare people the nuisance they have had to put up with for too long?

WITNEY CRICKET WEEK
We again saw W. G. Grace and the redoubtable Jessop in action this week.

WATER AT LAST

The water works is now finished. The tower as a whole is about as ugly a building as could have been erected. However we presume it was built for utility, and not withstanding its untoward appearance it sends us a good supply of water. The inscription on the tower has been painted. There appear the names of various councillors some of them who were not on the Council at the commencement of the work, and others who were not there at the finish. Surmounting the names is the representation of some animal; the body resembles a sheep, while the head is certainly more like a donkey. Is it possible that this is intended to represent the Witney Arms? If so we cannot congratulate the artist.

MESSENGER BOY PLEADS GUILTY TO BANGS

Harry Bridgewater of Woodgreen, telegraph messenger, was summoned for wantonly letting off a firework within 50 feet of the highway. The defendant pleaded guilty.
P.C. Baker stated that he saw the defendant at 7.30 on the night in question. He was letting off fireworks on Woodgreen. The witness took the remaining fireworks away from him
Supt Hawtin stated that he had received numerous complaints of boys letting off fireworks in the street. Ordered to pay costs 7/-.

THE MOP

The statute Mop was held here on Thursday. It being stock-market day there was a large attendance but very little hiring business was transacted. The pleasure attractions included:- Bailey's steam gondolas, the big wheel and Mr Ball's cinematograph exhibition. During the latter part of the day rain fell heavily, and this had the effect of sending people home earlier than usual, so trade was not as good as it would otherwise have been.

THE MOP IS NOT WHAT IT WAS

Alas! How its glories have fled since the days of my boyhood. Not only the presence of large numbers of men for the purpose of being hired, but hundreds of young girls, who stood in rows at various places in the street. Those who were willing to be their masters and mistresses passed in front of them scrutinizing their features and their form to see if they possessed the strength to undertake the "place". I have even heard that some mistresses would actually touch the girls in the ribs to see if they were in "good condition". My word how things have changed. A domestic servant does not now stand in the street waiting to be hired, she is now mistress of the position.

DEATH IN THE WORKHOUSE

On Tuesday there died at the Witney Union Workhouse an inmate named Fanny Clapton aged 83 years. who was admitted 73 years ago to the Northleigh Workhouse (at that time every parish had its own Workhouse). Soon afterwards the Union Workhouse was built and she was removed there, where she has been till she died. It has just been discovered that she has a relative at Northleigh, who thought that she had died 60 years ago. It has been calculated that it cost over £1000 to keep this woman in the Workhouse.

THE SCRUTATOR would like to know:

What is to be done to prevent a recurrence of the flooding scenes that have taken place this week at Standlake?
Whether the exceptionally wet weather is entirely responsible for this?
Whether there is some reason to believe that something might be done to remedy the flooding by attending to the drains?

WINTER SHOPPPING HOURS

The traders of the town have agreed to close as usual during the winter months as follows:-
Monday, Wednesday Thursday, Friday 7pm. Tuesdays 3pm. And Saturdays 9.30pm.

ODDFELLOWS' SUPPER

An occasional licence was granted to the Three Horse Shoes public house in Corn Street, on the occasion of the Oddfellows' Supper.

FIRE AT SALTMARSH AND DRUCE

At sometime past 3am Mrs Saltmarsh, on hearing falling slates, repaired to the bedroom over the kitchen where two of her children were sleeping. The fire had reached the room above the bedroom, and in a few minutes the children must have been suffocated. Mrs Saltmarsh took the children down the stairs and sent a messenger to the Captain of the Fire Brigade, who promptly turned out. Captain Green, seeing how serious the fire was, ran to the Town Hall and got out the portable engine, and with this tried to keep back the flames from the house. Soon the flames had reached the house and had also got hold of the adjoining premises belonging to Messrs Leigh and Son. Captain Green sent a messenger to call the Fire Brigade. Whether the messenger did not know who to call or some other cause it was not until Capt Green went to the engine house was the appliance got out. The result was the Brigade did not get water on to the fire for fifty minutes after the fire was discovered.

A hose was attached to a standpipe opposite "Friendly House" and taken up Messrs Leigh & Son's gateway, and from there two jets of water played on Leigh's premises, where not only was a considerable quantity of petroleum stored but there were 20 gallons of benzoline. As soon as possible this was poured down the drain and the petrol removed to a safe place.

The fire damage is estimated to be £2000.

SPEED LIMITS

The U.D.C. has been requested by the County Council to consider the following questions:-

1. Are there any roads on which motorcars should be prohibited or restricted?

Mr Knight thought that Mill Street should be prohibited as it was only 16 feet wide, and the corner was very dangerous.

Mr Knight's proposal was carried.

2. Are there any roads in the town on which the speed should be limited to 10mph?

The Council thought that all roads in the town should be so proscribed.

3. Are there any dangerous corners, crossroads, or precipitous places where the County Council should put up warning signs?

The U.D.C. considered signs should be put up as follows:

Top of Woodgreen Hill (denoting the crossroads at the bottom).

Newland by the Almshouses (denoting the same crossroads).

Mill Street at the top of the hill beyond Witney Mill.

Mill Street near the corner of High Street.

Town Hall (denoting Corn Street).

Station Road by cottages.

Station Road by corner near goods station.

To the Editor, Witney Gazette:

Dear Sir,

It would interest the inhabitants of Southleigh if they could be informed when the R.D.C. intend doing something to improve the road leading from the Village to the Station. At present it is in a shocking condition. It is true that sometime ago it was steamrolled, but the wet season, the overhanging trees and the uncut hedges have converted it into a mud-trench. It is impossible for Southleigh people to walk to the station without going over their boots in mud.

If the Council could get the trees cut and the road scraped they would confer a benefit on the Southleigh ratepayers.

Yours faithfully,

A Villager.

A DREAM

Through eating too much supper
before I went to bed
Strange thoughts came o'er my
slumbers, strange dreams came in my
head
The world seemed topsy-turvy, and
the people of renown
Were doing most peculiar things,
when the world turned upside down.

Now Witney has a Council who in
committee sit.
I thought that they were drainers that
knew a little bit,
But my dreams came in my slumbers,
I must surely take a pill
For I dreamed that the Witney
Council made their drains run up hill.

I dreamt they made a water tower, and
so gained great renown
And they thought they'd put their
names up, if it only cost a crown
But since I've woke from dreaming I
Don't know what to say
For they call upon the ratepayer
To pay – and pay – and pay.

THE HUNTING QUESTION

The man who dislikes to see the hounds come along his way attended by gaily dressed horse-men and horse-women is in my opinion a poor creature. I warrant if the innermost recesses of such a one's life were ferreted out, it would be found that as a man and a citizen he was no better than he should be. I have nothing to say here about the cruelty of the sport, because if I were to begin speaking on such a subject, I would have to bring in the wickedness of fishing and a hundred other matters of a kindred nature, which meet disapproval from no one.

Yes, I cannot doubt foxhunting plays a very important part in modern life, and therefore it must have an influence for good or for evil upon several classes of people in this country. As I think it tends in the main for good, I like to see it well supported.

BREAD AND BEEF CHARITY

As usual large quantities of bread and beef were given away by the Bailiffs (Messrs R.L.Walker and W. R .Payne). In total 1ton 15 cwt of beef and 700 loaves of bread.

THE FIRE BRIGADE

Mr F.M.Green who has been Captain of the Witney Fire Brigade for several years has resigned in consequence of his numerous engagements. Mr Herbert Smith has consented to be the new Captain.

****

WOODMAN SPARE THAT AXE

Sometime ago the U.D.C. authorised a member of the Committee to trim some trees overhanging Station Road, after obtaining consent from the owners. Well, there is no doubt that the trees have been trimmed, but what do the owners think of the work? Never probably, has anyone seen such destruction to the beauty of the entrance to the town. But what is more important still is how the majestic elms near the passenger station are going to be treated. It appears that the Committee in question intend to submit these ornaments to the town to the same kind of treatment as those further up the road. We should say with all the emphasis at our command "Woodman spare that tree".

As a result of an appeal by the Witney Gazette the topping of trees near the railway station was stopped. We should like to know what right the Witney Council had to lop the trees on Station Hill. It is just possible that they might have had the power to lop those overhanging the road; even that is somewhat doubtful in the case of these trees. The Station Hill road is repairable by the Railway Company and the Council have nothing to do with it. However when once the vandalic spirit gets the upper hand, it is difficult to stay its destructiveness.

SAINT MARY'S SCHOOL PRIZES

The following received prizes.
Rector's Prize: H. Monk, A. Clinkard, L. Long, H. Richards, F, Brooks, W. Horne.

Rev. C. W. Jenkyn prize:
J. Burford, F. Buckingham, G. Sherbourne.
Rev. M. S. Newland prize:
H. Ferriman, G. Burford, W. Fowler, W. Sherbourne.
Mr Hayter's prize:
J. Burford, A. Nicklen, G. Probetts, G. Harris, S. Collis, J. Warner, H. Simpson, Herbert Halay.

CANON FOXLEY NORRIS TO LEAVE US

The Rector has resigned the living after nearly a quarter of a century of faithful work during which he has been ably assisted by his wife and the Misses Norris.

We are quite sure that our readers will very sincerely regret to hear this news. Not only was the Rev. gentleman a most eloquent preacher and in every way a model clergyman, but he was also an excellent townsman. What ever has been done for the welfare of Witney during the past twenty years has always had his hearty support. Whoever is appointed to succeed him in this important office will have hard work to fill the gap which his severance from Witney will cause.

TRAP ACCIDENT

As Mr H.Hollis of High Coggs was driving home on Saturday night, when near the County Court in Bridge Street, a brake containing some Woodstock footballers suddenly turned round and ran into Mr. Hollis, with the result that he, and some young ladies that were with him, were all thrown out. Fortunately no one was seriously injured.

****

1904

In February a crippling Japanese raid on the Russian fleet started war between the two countries. The Russians were overwhelmed by the superior technology, including wireless communications, of their opponents. Sympathies here were very much on the side of the Japanese, in fact there was a craze for all things Japanese, as the highly successful Japanese Fair held in Witney in November shows.

King Edward's diplomatic initiative was successful in bringing about the signing of the Entente Cordiale with France in April. Long-standing disputes were settled, and a lasting and generally popular friendship was established.

Water became even more important in the daily life of Witney citizens. Flooding in February caused problems for householders and more serious ones for farmers. Worse - the new Water Tower proved to be an expensive failure, fit only to inspire satirical poems.

Canon Foxley Norris retired, and was replaced as Rector by the Rev James Barker Kirby, who immediately settled into his parish work. He readily agreed to rent The Leys to the Council, thereby providing the town with a large recreation ground.

The Education Act of 1902 was having repercussions. Some highly respectable Nonconformist residents became Passive Resisters: they refused to pay a portion of the poor rate because it covered sectarian teaching in schools, including Roman Catholic ones, which they could not support. They were summoned, and the resulting court case, seizure of goods and auction make extraordinary reading.

NEW YEAR WISHES

The Witney Gazette wishes all its readers a Happy and Prosperous New Year. 1904 marks the newspaper's 21st anniversary. Our editorial policy has always been one of independence: the fact that both political parties have complained shows that we have adhered to it faithfully!

BIRTHDAY CELEBRATIONS

Mr. C. Early J.P. has recently reached the age of 79. Celebrations at his residence in Newland included fireworks and a huge bonfire.

SERIOUS ASSAULT CHARGES

At Petty Sessions two labourers were charged with assaulting a policeman and stealing his truncheon and whistle, value 10/-, in Dark Lane. The P.C. alleged that the accused knocked him down several times, threw him in the ditch and took the truncheon and whistle. The accused men and their wives alleged that they had found the constable drunk in the ditch, and had confiscated the truncheon for safety reasons. The case was dismissed.

SUICIDE TRAGEDY

The funeral has taken place of a respected and popular farmer and cattle dealer, aged 45. He had suffered a sudden attack of mania, which caused him to have hallucinations and to believe that he was being persecuted by people who were in reality, his friends. He took his own life by cutting his throat at home.

THUNDERSTORM

On January 13 a great storm with vivid lightning and gale-force winds gave Witney one of the roughest nights of recent years. Fortunately little damage is reported.

DEATH OF OLDEST INHABITANT

Mr Robert ('Bobby') Taylor, bootmaker, of Bridge Street, has died at the age of 98. Born in 1805, he lived in Witney all his life. He could remember the funeral of Queen Caroline and Queen Victoria's coronation. Until quite recently he could be seen taking his usual brisk walks round the town.

LIVING CHESS

The Young Women's Social Club organised a most unusual entertainment: members dressed in Red and White Chess costumes were placed on a huge 'Chessboard' in the Corn Exchange. After a musical and dancing introduction, Mr. W. Derby Hyde and Mr. W. Smith Jun. played a game of chess. Mr Smith won. More music and dancing followed, including numbers by Wright's Quadrille Band.

WESLEYAN JUVENILE MISSIONARIES

At the annual tea for the Juvenile Collectors, the Chairman and all the speakers were juveniles. Master Owen Dring took the chair. Among the speakers were Miss Emily Walford as a Chinese girl and Master Harold Harris as a Pariah boy. The young people had collected £37.17.9d, £10 more than last year.

LADYSMITH EXPERIENCES

The Rev. O. Spencer Watkins addressed a large audience at the Wesleyan School on his experiences during the Siege of Ladysmith, where his duties as a Chaplain consisted of visiting the wounded and burying the dead. He gave dramatic descriptions of the horrors of battle, the bravery of the troops, and the boredom and privations of life under siege.

SOAKING WEATHER

Since the beginning of the year about three and a half inches of rain has fallen. Flooded fields have delayed planting locally, and young lambs have been lost. The agricultural outlook is a gloomy one. In Witney, heavy rain has caused flooding in gardens, and householders on Bridge Street have prepared barricades, which luckily have not been needed.

RUSSO-JAPANESE WAR

We congratulate the plucky little Japanese on their opening success in the war, which has just broken out. Japan has become one of the most advanced nations in the world, while Russia is governed by a despotism, which is a disgrace to the times in which we live.

MUD AND POTHOLES

Witney's streets are in a wretched state, with holes in Corn Street and High Street caused by the drainage work. Worse still, the Council persists in the idiotic system of scraping the mud into heaps at the side of the roadway, and leaving it there for days for the unwary to walk into. It is high time something was done to improve the situation.

DRINK PETITION

A petition to the Licensing Authorities was presented by Mr C.W.Early, with a number of clergy and prominent citizens, and signed by 1029 persons over sixteen, requesting that fewer licences for the sale of intoxicating liquor should be granted in the area. A similar petition was delivered last year. It pointed out that in Liverpool a reduction in licences granted had been followed by a huge reduction in prosecutions for drunkenness. In London there was one 'on' licence per 446 inhabitants, in Birmingham one to 290, in Sheffield one to 270, but in Witney one to 130 - a proportion greatly in excess of the requirements of the population. The Chairman said the Bench would go into the matter next year.

AFFILIATION CASES

A Woodgreen man was ordered to pay 2/- a week to a New Yatt woman, and a Somertown man who admitted paternity of a Minster woman's child was ordered to pay 1/6 a week and costs.

SOCIAL TEA

The annual event of a parochial tea has been revived by the Ladies of the Church Needlework Society. Over 200 people sat down to tea, and enjoyed a sale of work in aid of the Church School Fund. Among highlights of the entertainment which followed were a recitation, 'The Bishop and the Caterpillar', by Dr Batt, and the song, 'Spring is Coming', by Miss Gleave.

WATER TOWER FIASCO

On February 25 the huge tank on the Water Tower, built less than six months ago, burst and was left reduced to a shapeless mass streaming with water. A large crowd soon collected to wonder at this disaster. Someone must be to blame, and even the long-suffering ratepayers of Witney would resent having to pay a penny towards putting it right. At least the town's water supply is not affected: the water is now being pumped directly into the mains instead of the tank. The dimensions of the ill-fated tank are as follows: Depth 13ft 6in; Length 31ft; Breadth 31ft; Capacity 80,000gals. The names of the Urban District Councillors appear on a plaque at the foot of the Tower.

Water Tower,
Tank on top,
Filled with water
Went off pop.

Sudden strain,
Sides bent,
Consequently
Big rent.

Losing water,
Like a crock,
To the Council
Quite a shock.

Great sensation,
Council run,
And people too,
To see the fun.

Poor little lambs,
With names below,
So proudly raised,
Dishonoured so.

It's not our fault
Perhaps they'll say
But who will have
To pay pay pay?

BL

PASSIVE RESISTERS

A Primitive Methodist minister and nine other men were summoned for non-payment of a portion of the poor rate. They explained that they were law-abiding citizens, but that their position as workers in the various Free Churches precluded them from paying for sectarian teaching in the schools. This would mean that they would have to support Roman Catholic schools, which was against their principles as citizens and Christians. The Chairman said he had to make an order for the rate to be paid, but the Bench agreed that one distress warrant might be issued for the whole of the defendants.

GOODS SEIZED The Passive Resisters mentioned above have had some of their goods seized. Two Overseers with a van went to their houses, where they were courteously received, and took possession of goods including fish knives, a watch-chain, chairs and clocks. The articles were kept at the Police Station and sold after five days, the rate still remaining unpaid.

AN UNUSUAL AUCTION At the sale, the Auctioneer began by saying that he was conducting his business on a non-profit-making basis, as his sympathies were with the Passive Resisters. Many of those present agreed with him, and all the items fetched more than enough to pay the debts. The proceedings ended with cheers for the Auctioneer, the Police and the Overseers.

WATER TOWER

A Committee has been formed to get expert advice with reference to the disaster at the Water Tower.

TEACHERS NEEDED

Vacancies are advertised for fifty TEACHERS. Salaries: Male, £60 to £75 per annum; Female, £50 to £60. Annual Increments £2.10s. Previous experience may be taken into account. Apply: The Education Secretary, Cambridge Street, Aylesbury.

POPULAR GUARD RETIRES

Guard Brown, well-known for his helpfulness and courtesy to rich and poor alike, has retired from the Witney and Fairford Railway after 25 years' service.

DIPHTHERIA AT STANDLAKE

The overflowing drains at Standlake are being blamed for causing outbreaks of diphtheria. Prompt action is needed.

VILLAGE READING ROOM

The Vicar of Minster Lovell writes to appeal for donations to set up a Reading Room to brighten and strengthen the lives of sober, honest, respectable and earnest men - but poor.

NEW RECTOR

We can announce the name of the newly-appointed Rector of Witney, who will replace Canon Foxley Norris as from May 1st. He is the Rev James Barker Kirby, who has served curacies at Reading and Buckingham, and as Vicar of Wooburn, Bucks, a manufacturing town not unlike Witney. He has a Cambridge degree in Law Honours (2nd class) and was ordained Priest in 1889.

We have it on good authority that Mr Kirby is in the prime of life, and is exactly the man for the place. Witney people, with their usual urbanity, will give him a hearty welcome, and we venture to remark that it will be his own fault if he does not get on cordially with them.

ANOTHER EARLY COMES OF AGE

Mr Edward C.Early, second son of Mr and Mrs J.V.Early, celebrated his 21st birthday with a substantial meat tea for some 400 persons, held upstairs at the Wesleyan Schools. His gift from the employees at the Mill was a handsome dressing and suit case, with silver fittings, presented by Mr Charles Haley, who has worked for the firm for 61 years. After congratulating the young master, Mr Haley recalled hard times when tuckers and spinners of Witney had to 'break stones in the market house' to earn a little to support them. Now, he said, the blanket business was steadily improving. He hoped many others would rival his work record, remarking (to applause) that a rolling stone gathers no moss.

TRAMPS SENTENCED

At Petty Sessions a married couple, both tramps, were charged with sleeping rough and neglecting their four children. A policeman described finding the family sleeping in a shed. The children, aged between 2 and 11 years, were wet through and dirty. They were taken to the Workhouse, where they were found to be verminous and suffering from chilblains and swollen feet. The parents, who have previous convictions, were sentenced to prison, the father to six weeks and the mother to three. Three other tramps were sentenced to 14 days' hard labour for refusing to carry out the task of picking 4lbs of oakum at Witney Union Workhouse.

WHAT IS A DEACONESS?

The Rev T.B. Stephenson gave an illustrated lecture on 'A Deaconess, what is she? What does she?' He said that after a slow start, there were now 1,200 Deaconesses in various countries. They had erected chapels, hospitals and schools, and were also trained in nursing. A collection was taken up in aid of the local Deaconess Fund.

54

HALF-HOLIDAY PETITION

Shop assistants in Witney have asked their employers for a proper weekly half-holiday. At present, shops close at 3pm on Tuesdays. The assistants would like closing time to be changed to one or two o'clock. As little trade is done after midday on Tuesdays this request does not seem unreasonable, but the traders have not seen fit to agree to it.

BAD LANGUAGE

At petty sessions, a man and woman (not husband and wife) summoned each other for using obscene and abusive language at the same time and place. Both were ordered to pay 7/- costs.

AFRICA IN SONG AND STORY

Mr J. H. Balmer and Miss Elsie Clark and their four Kaffir Boys (two of them very small) gave a most enjoyable entertainment. First, Mr. Balmer showed a large map of Africa and described the vast territory, which is now under British rule. Those who knew that splendid country best, he said, knew how to value it, unlike some who went there for a short time and gave it a bad name. Miss Clark also spoke, alluding particularly to the degraded position of the native women. The Boys then showed their versatility with a wide selection of songs both sentimental and comic, some with lively action and some in the Kaffir tongue. They were received with rapturous applause.

DEATH OF MR W PAINE

The town has lost one of its principal personalities, Mr. W. Paine, who has died at the ripe age of 81. He started his carrier's business in Witney in 1850, long before many of today's traders were born. In 1861, when the Witney Railway was opened, he was appointed goods agent, and his waggon was a familiar and welcome sight around the town and villages. He was in business for 40 years, earning the respect and appreciation of all who knew him.

CLOCK LIGHTING

The Council has accepted the tender of the Gas Company to light the Butter Cross clock for nine months for £4 5s 6d. A motion to light it for 12 months, to include the summer, was defeated.

PRESENTATION TO RETIRING RECTOR

The resignation of Canon Foxley Norris from his position as Rector has been marked by the presentation of a testimonial in the form of a purse, with illuminated address and list of subscribers, for which £165 was collected.

The testimonial was presented privately because of the illness of both the Canon and his wife. It expressed regret at his retirement after 25 years of devoted service, and assured him of the appreciation and gratitude of his parishioners. In a letter to the Gazette, the Canon said he hoped to make grateful acknowledgements to all the contributors. This would take some time, as they numbered three or four hundred.

WHITHER THE WORKHOUSE?

A new boiler is to be installed at the Workhouse, at a cost of £1500. The old one has lasted well, having been put in 70 years ago when the Workhouse was first built. At that time provision was made for 450 inmates; at present there are only 106 indoor paupers in occupation. Perhaps it will not be long before this awkwardly constructed building becomes obsolete. Some day perhaps the deserving poor will receive old age pensions to enable them to live in their own houses. Childrens' homes will be provided too. Lazy vagabonds will either starve or go into some kind of establishment more after the nature of a prison.

TUBERCULOSIS FROM ANIMALS

A Royal Commission has unanimously concluded that, contrary to previous theories, tuberculosis can be transmitted from animals to human beings, and vice versa. Until legislation prevents diseased animals and their products from being sold to the public, householders should boil their milk. There is no more reason in drinking raw milk than there is in eating raw beef.

BEAUTY AND NEGLECT

How many of the inhabitants of Witney value, as they should do, the really beautiful approach to the town from the Railway Station? First of all stand the mighty elms which flank the Leys, notwithstanding 'Vandals' attack upon them last autumn; and then the avenue of beautiful limes, with foliage brightest green; while nearer the town is the lovely walk through the Churchyard, with its wild but beautiful scenery of shrubs, flowers and trees on either hand.

Regrettably, some of the forest trees have grown so rapidly that they are in danger of not only hiding the Church but even damaging its foundations. Smaller ornamental trees should be planted in their places, and the lower branches of the limes should be lopped. At present they leave no room for walkers to put up their umbrellas in wet weather. As for the Churchyard, many of the tombstones are so dilapidated as to be a disgrace to all concerned.

****

NOTICE: Ten shillings reward will be paid for the names of three cyclists (a woman and two men) who were the cause of an accident to a motor-cyclist and lady in trailer, on the road near Ducklington Mill in the afternoon of Whit-Sunday last. Super-intendent Hawtin, Witney, or F.F. Paxman, Tewkesbury.

NEW RECTOR

The institution of the new Rector of Witney, the Rev J. Barber Kirby M.A., was carried out by the Lord Bishop of Oxford.

At a Vestry meeting at St. Mary's Church, the new Rector expressed appreciation and gratitude for the welcome and help he had received, stressing in particular his desire for a cordial and co-operative relationship with the Nonconformists of the town. Rev Kirby also paid tribute to the retiring Rector and wished him long life in his time of rest.

ARSONIST CAUGHT AT LAST

A man was sentenced to 4 years' penal servitude for setting fire to a hayrick in Clanfield. He had been strongly suspected of other fires, but proof was lacking. On this occasion a policeman was watching the rickyard and saw the accused striking matches and throwing them into the rick. The culprit's case was not improved by his attempting to throw blame on another man.

HAPPY HAYMAKING

Unlike last June, when hay was seen floating on flooded fields, the present genial weather is much appreciated by farmers. The hay crop is well above average in quality and quantity. It is gratifying to learn that the Duke of Marlborough has remitted 10% of his tenants' rents, to show his sympathy for last year's disastrous losses.

RAILWAY IMPROVEMENT

The Great Western Railway Company has constructed new sidings at Witney and Bampton stations. They are a great convenience to those having business in the goods yards, and will save many hours of valuable time.

THE LAMENT OF THE WATER TANK

Oh! All who pass by
Cast a pitying eye
Where 'twixt Tower and sky,
My sides all awry
I mourn and I sigh
For the days now gone by,
When my aim was to try
The Town to supply.

If you can squeeze a tear
Do pray drop it here -
For greatly I fear,
From what I can hear,
It will take quite a year
To put me in gear.

My tears overflow,
When I glance down below
And see the brave show,
(on the tablet, you know)
Of the Council who throw
Such scorn on me now.

No more can I say,
Such grief doth me sway -
One comforting ray
Shines on me today -
I shall have nothing to pay,
Though the rate-payers may.

ROYAL MEETING

The King's visit to Germany is a happy omen for the future peace of the world. The ruler of the Nation with the most powerful navy in the world meets the ruler of the greatest army in Europe, and side by side they pledge each other to peace. Long may the two flags fly peacefully together, and what is more, may they influence other nations in that happy direction.

MUCH REDUCED LIVING

The living of Witney has gone down to £370 nett, according to the Parish Magazine. 25 years ago it was over £2000. Tithes are now little more than half the value they were then. The clergy have suffered badly from the agricultural depression, and yet they do not complain, knowing that their poverty is for the benefit of the country at large.

PERFECT ATTENDANCE

John Burford, a pupil of St Mary's Boys' National School, has been presented with a silver watch for never being absent or late during his 10 years and 10 months at the school. He has made nearly 5000 consecutive attendances, and is the first boy in the county to receive such a reward.

FEAST ON THE LEYS?

The Council plans to approach the Rector to ask for fairs, the Feast, circuses etc to be held on the Leys rather than Church Green, where they cause noise and incon-venience to residents.

YOUNG DELINQUENTS

A boy aged seven was fined 20/- and sentenced to six strokes of the rod for setting fire to two hayricks and one straw rick at Eynsham.
Two Minster lads were fined 10/- each, with costs of 6/- and damage 3/9d, for throwing stones at telegraph posts and damaging insulators.

BICYCLE ACCIDENT

A serious accident has befallen Miss Webb, a teacher at the Wesleyan Schools. Descending Woodgreen Hill, she lost control of her bicycle, dashed over the pavement and was thrown with great force against the wall of a house. She sustained a severe cut to the forehead and another to the back of the head. Dr Kelly was soon in attendance. Miss Webb has regained consciousness and is now progressing favourably.

BOYS' BRIGADE CAMP

The 1st Company Witney Boys' Brigade spent a very successful week camping on Hayling Island. Many of the boys had never seen the open sea before, and much enjoyed bathing parades and picnics on the beach. On Sunday morning they marched to Church Parade at the Independent Chapel, headed by the Band. That evening they also had a Camp Service. High point of the week was a visit to Portsmouth to see Nelson's Victory and the Great Dockyard, where they had a conducted tour of the battleship HMS Caesar.

FOR SALE. – BATH CHAIR, with hood; four bicycle wheels; rubber tyres; for shafts or handle. Apply C. *Gazette* Office, Witney

RECORD TEMPERATURES

Sunday July 22nd was the hottest day in Witney for some years. At 2pm the temperature was 131 degrees Fahrenheit in the sun and 98 degrees in the shade. At sunset it was 80 degrees.

WORKHOUSE OUTING

The inmates of the Workhouse spent an enjoyable afternoon at Ringwood as guests of Mr and Mrs J. W. Abraham. They travelled in vans loaned by Witney traders. After strolling in the beautiful gardens they were served a substantial tea of beef, ham, bread and butter and cake. Later there was dancing and an impromptu concert, with biscuits, beer, lemonade and snuff ad lib. At the close of the day an inmate named Daniels thanked the hosts and helpers for their kindness.

PORTSMOUTH STILL POPULAR

This year's Witney Trip was to Portsmouth, which proved a popular and exciting visit in spite of comments that it has perhaps figured rather too frequently as a destination. The Witney Trips were started in 1879 by the late Mr E Smitheman, Station Master. It is true that out of 24 Trips Portsmouth has been chosen ten times, including this year. However, a good time was had by all. Extra, but unwelcome, excitement was felt by some trippers who witnessed the disastrous fire on the South Parade Pier.

CHURCH WORK DEBTS

At a meeting called by the Rector, Rev J.B. Kirby, it was decided to appeal for donations to clear the £400 owed by the parish. Gifts amounting to £260 have already been pledged, and September's Fete should provide the rest.

MOTOR CAR ACCIDENT

Mr Norman Bayles, a visitor to the town, was taking three ladies for a drive through Cokethorpe Park in his 20 horse power car, when it suddenly slipped on the wet road, and somersaulted into a ditch. One lady was thrown over the hedge, and Mr Bayles and another lady were pinned to the earth by the seats of the car. Luckily they were extricated by Messrs Jones and taken into Cokethorpe House. Medical aid was summoned by telephone. Though Mr Bayles was delirious, he and his passengers were not seriously injured.

NEW SCHOOL BUILDINGS NEEDED

The Inspectors' report on the Grammar and Technical School praises the standard of teaching, but warns that for real efficiency the school needs a new wing consisting of two classrooms, an art room and a manual workshop, as well as new dormitories for the boarding department.

After distributing the prizes, the Rector asked his audience to clear from their minds for the moment all ideas about passive resistence and theological controversy, and get back to more fundamental ideas about education. This meant the developing on the right lines of those intellectual, spiritual and physical powers with which the child was endowed by God; to train for life and not for a special occupation. Fortunately the idea that the function of teachers was to cram information into young minds in order to pass examinations and please examiners was being replaced by sounder conceptions of the relationship between teachers and pupils. If children were not taught to prefer the good, the beautiful and the true to the bad, the ugly and the false, their education had fallen short of what it should be.

DROWNING TRAGEDY

An inquest was told that Reginald Luckett, aged 12, went swimming in the river at Minster Lovell with two friends, at a spot unfamiliar to them, where the water was deep and weedy. Though Reginald could swim a little, he soon got into difficulties, and his friends' efforts to save him failed. The Jury gave their fees towards a wreath to be laid on the poor boy's grave. The Vicar has suggested that a shallow portion of the river should be fenced off for bathing purposes.

NEGLECTED ROAD

The roadway leading from Corn Street and The Crofts to the Station is still in a disgraceful state, with loose stones, almost as big as one's head, covering the surface over which the long-suffering inhabitants have to pick their way as best they can. Presumably Council members do not generally take their walks in what has become a much-frequented promenade, or surely something would have been done about it by now.

PLANS FOR THE LEYS

The Rector has agreed to rent the Leys to the Council for £20 per annum, and has even agreed to waive £12 of the first year's rent. The Council has thus acquired a recreation ground which can also accommodate fairs. This is a great advantage. Not only is there more space, but the heavy electric and steam machinery needed to run the switchback, galloping horses and cinematograph shows will no longer cause damage to the grass on Church Green, so recently renovated at great cost by the Council.

AUTO-CYCLE THRILLS

There was great excitement in Witney when the competitors in the 1000 miles tour, organised by the Auto Cycle Club, passed through the town. The object of the tour was to test the reliability of various motor cycles. The fifth day's route was from Doncaster to Oxford via Nottingham, Leicester, Cheltenham and Witney. A crowd in Market Square greeted the first arrivals, among whom was F.W.Chase on his celebrated hill-climbing Chase MotorCycle. The riders left Doncaster at 7.30am; all had arrived in Oxford by 8.45pm.

MUSHROOM THIEVES

Two 15-year-old boys were fined 7/- each for stealing 7lbs of cultivated mushrooms on enclosed land.

CRUELTY TO FOWLS

A grocer from Cogges was fined 15/- for cruelly ill-treating 22 fowls. The birds were tied together tightly in twos and taken to market in a crate which was too small.

FIREMEN'S OUTING

The Volunteer Fire Brigade spent a happy afternoon at Bablockhythe in splendid weather. They played a cricket match with a team of gentlemen camping in the vicinity. The Campers won. After tea the firemen and campers had a pleasant and accident-free row on the river in half a dozen boats. A capital supper, songs and speeches concluded a highly successful outing.

THE BATTLE OF BRIDEWELL

The peace of Bridewell Farm, near Northleigh, was shattered by the crack of rifle and the booming of cannon when the 'F' Company (Witney) Volunteers and the 'I' Company Oxford Cyclists held a sham battle. The Cyclists' mission was to intercept a convoy taking essential supplies to 'F' Company at Bridewell. However, they lost their way and were ambushed by their foes on the ridge. All guns were silenced while tea was taken on Mr Gask's lawn, where quite a bevy of the fair sex were only too happy to wait on them. Battle then resumed, with murderous rifle fire and a fixed bayonet charge. After more refreshments, the warriors all departed.

PARISH FETE

The new Rector, Rev J.B. Kirby, has made enormous efforts to clear the £400 debt, which has hung over the parish for several years. At a meeting in August, £250 was raised from enthusiastic supporters. To supplement this, a fete was organised for September 6. The weather was fine, and nearly 1000 persons enjoyed the event on the Rectory lawn. Comic sketches were performed by talented amateurs, and tea was served in relays by lady helpers. Attractions included a golf putting competition, a flower stall and a phonograph.

The most popular event was the Bicycle Gymkhana, a novelty in Witney. Obstacle races for both gentleman and lady cyclists provided thrills, and the costume races, egg and ladle race and tortoise race caused much hilarity. The prettiest race was the 'Tandem', in which two ladies on decorated bicycles with reins attached to them rode round the course with a gentleman riding behind and holding the reins.

The Rector was thanked for presenting the prizes, and Mrs Kirby for her hard work on the organising side. In the evening a dance was held at the Corn Exchange.

SCHOOL CLOSURES

Standlake School has only been open for 19 weeks in the last 12 months. Infectious diseases have caused the closures. The school should be reopened as soon as it has been properly disinfected.

FEASTING ON THE LEYS

Many people arrived by train to visit relatives and enjoy the excitement of Witney Feast on The Leys. The Sunday services were heartily supported. In the evening people visiting the site were astonished to see more than a hundred horses belonging to the showmen pastured on The Leys. Unfortunately it rained heavily on the Monday, but attendance picked up on the Tuesday. A few residents deplored what they saw as a break with tradition in abandoning Church Green, but we point out that the Green has by no means always been the Fair's location, and that The Leys provides much more space as well as saving the Green from damage.

VANDALS UNPUNISHED

Three boys have been taken to court for stealing apples from gardens, but other boys, youths and even young men who should know better are shamelessly pulling down railings and damaging walls, fences, gates and stiles. Why are they not prosecuted? The Constabulary should act, and parents should not shirk their responsibility for their children's moral training.

NEW HYMN BOOK

On September 11th the new Methodist Hymn Book was used for the first time at the Wesleyan Chapel.

MILK will be sold from the cart at TWO PENCE PER QUART, for cash only, commencing October 10th. Regular customers in the town will be waited on as usual. R.D. Buswell, Burwell Farm. [advert]

MOP FAIR

At the annual hiring fair little hiring seemed to take place. Young men and maidens apparently do not care to stand in the market for inspection, but make use of the advertising columns of a newspaper instead. A considerable number of county people, however, as usual visited the town, and ample provision was made for their entertainment on the Witney Recreation Ground. There were Ball's animated picture show, Bailey's switchback and art show; shooting shows of various kinds, sweet stalls, fancy goods etc, and all the usual fun of the fair was kept going till near midnight. It seemed rather strange to see the streets and the Green so empty on a fair night, but on the whole most people seemed to like the new arrangement and all passed off in a most orderly manner.

A FAMILY QUARREL

Two brothers of Eynsham, both shoemakers, were summoned for committing a breach of the peace. P.C. Parker stated that they were fighting in the street with their coats off at 10.30pm, and one swore at him when he asked them to stop. Though a sister-in-law alleged that the policeman was the only person she heard using bad language, they were both fined 10s for fighting, with an extra 10s fine for the brother who swore.

SIR WILLIAM HARCOURT

The death has occurred, at the age of 77, of Sir William Harcourt. He was laid to rest on October 7th in the family vault in Nuneham Park. Sir William had a most distinguished political career. He served for many years as M.P. for Oxford, and among the Government posts he held under Mr Gladstone were Solicitor General, Home Secretary and Chancellor of the Exchequer.

PROBLEM OF VAGABONDS

The recent brutal murder and robbery of an inoffensive traveller, a carpenter aged 29, is a terrible indictment against our present day civilisation.

Our cherished principle of the liberty of the subject means that it is very difficult to deal with the problem of violent, thieving tramps when there are also perfectly respectable men travelling in search of work. The children of tramps and gypsies pose another serious question: how can compulsory education benefit them when they are always on the move?

SUNDAY DISTURBANCES

Some local lads (and girls too) have been causing noisy disturbances in the area between the Butter Cross and the Railway Station. On Sunday nights in the Churchyard the shouting, screaming and bad language have been disgraceful. The fact that the Churchyard lamp has not been alight recently may well be significant. Why, when the Police Station is so near, is this disorderly conduct not stopped?

THE LEYS LEASE

At a meeting of the Urban District Council, the seal of the Council was affixed to a lease of The Leys to the Council by the Rector for 21 years, the Council to have the option of terminating the same at the end of 14 years

LOST, - at Witney Market, on October 20th, a small SPOTTED PIG. Finders will be rewarded, and any person detaining the pig after this notice will be prosecuted. Frank Walker, Freeland, Eynsham.

EXOTIC WESLEYAN BAZAAR

A two-day Japanese Fair and Bazaar was held to raise funds to cover the recent repairs and renovations at the Wesleyan Schools. As well as the usual stalls selling refreshments, needlework, flowers and fruit, there was a Japanese Room with a fish pond and Japanese fancy goods for sale. The hall was beautifully decorated with lanterns and umbrellas, and the stalls were draped with Japanese figured cloth and surmounted with pagodas.

Helpers in kimonos charmed the visitors. One side show consisted of living waxworks, including Old Father Time and the Babes in the Wood. There was a shooting gallery and art exhibition. Most delightful of all was the parade of 25 Little Japs in pretty costumes. Concerts were held each evening. The proceeds amounted to £290, a breathtaking total that reflected the hard work of the ladies and gentlemen who organised the event.

BICYCLE LAMP THEFT

Two boys, aged 12 and 9, pleaded guilty to stealing a bicycle lamp. They were ordered to pay 9/- each. The 12-year-old received five strokes of the birch rod, and the 9-year-old received three.

***

TELEPHONIC IMPROVEMENTS

We hear that the National Telephonic Company are energetically canvassing with a view of extending the telephonic connection in the Witney area. Several of the leading tradesmen have intimated their desire for such communication, and it only remains for the residents in the neighbourhood to take the matter up, to secure an efficient local service. The rates are fixed at about half the usual sum.

FOOTBALL AT READING

A special 1pm train left Witney for Reading, carrying enthusiasts to the Reading v Southampton football match. Mr Herbert Smith, of the Witney Smith family, is Captain of Reading, so the Witney group were delighted with the biscuit town's 2-0 win.

GENTLEMAN going abroad wishes to dispose of £15 15s Rudge Whitworth BICYCLE; 2 speed gear; equal to new; £11 10s - Seen at Eaton & Sons, Witney.

INFIRMARY APPEAL

An urgent special appeal for funds for the Radcliffe Infirmary has been launched. This institution is an immense boon to the poorer classes, whose appreciation is shown in the Hospital collections made by Friendly Societies in Witney, Bampton and other places. The question that arises is whether those more fortunately situated than those who derive a direct benefit from the Infirmary do as much as they can for this excellent county Institution.

NURSE FUND CHANGES

At an important meeting of the subscribers to the Witney Trained Nurse Fund, it was unanimously decided to change the name to The Witney Nursing Association, and to widen the basis of management to include all townspeople without regard to religious denomination. Tribute was paid to Mrs Batt as honorary secretary and to Nurse Sutton for her valuable nursing services.

WEATHER FACTS

After a memorably long and pleasant summer, lasting until November, we now have 20 degrees of frost and a couple of inches of snow on the ground. Old people are, however unanimous in declaring that a severe November means a mild winter.

The fall of snow has produced the usual uncomfortable state of things in Witney; pathways unswept, slides everywhere on the paths, until locomotion has become absolutely dangerous.

WEALTHY WITNEY?

There was a time when Witney was spoken of as a poverty-stricken town. This can scarcely be said to be the case now. There is abundant evidence all around pointing to prosperity at the present time. The most recent proof is in the fact that the Wesleyan Japanese Fair realised the large sum of £290. This, taken with another equally successful function in connection with the Church recently, tends to show that Witney, although rated at nearly 10/-, is not exactly in a hopeless state of poverty.

SPORT DEBATED

At the Church of England Men's Society Mr W. Smith, J.P., referred to cricket, football, billiards, cards, shooting etc. as activities tending to bring out the best qualities of young men, such as endurance, self-denial, courage and perseverance. Even horse-racing he would not object to if it could be done without gambling. In the subsequent discussion the prevailing opinion was that field sports, excepting stag hunting, did not entail unnecessary pain, and that gambling, in any shape, degraded sport, and should be avoided.

ILLEGAL FISHING

Three Ducklington men were fined 10/- each for illegally snaring fish with poles and wires in water whose fishing rights are held by Captain Buller and Mr E. Strange.

THEFT OF SPIRITS

A Corn Street woman was found guilty of stealing a bottle of brandy, one of rum, two of gin and one of whisky from the Eagle Tavern, the value of the spirits being 16/-. She was fined £1 with a fortnight to pay.

TEMPERANCE MEETING

Addressing a large audience at the Wesleyan Schools, the Rev H.T. Meakin said that now that unintoxicating wine was used for Communion in the majority of Wesleyan Chapels, he believed the time would come when all the Wesleyan Chapels would become great centres of temperance; further than that he believed the time would come when the whole Church of God would be teetotal. For himself, he considered it would be a sin for him to take an intoxicating drink. He deplored the fact that commissions, reports and Bills had repeatedly failed to stimulate Parliamentary action to curb the drunkenness which was steadily increasing everywhere. He was in favour of abandoning approaches to Parliament, and instead organising a great pledge-signing campaign to multiply the number of total abstainers.

SPECIAL SERVICE FOR MEN

At a special service for men held in Holy Trinity Church in connection with the Witney Church of England Men's Society, the Rev J. Kinchin Smith took for his text I John ii, 'I have written unto you young men because you are strong.' He stressed that strength was needed not only in the body and mind, but in the soul as well.

CHARITIES

The Bailliffs distributed bread and beef to some 650 recipients, and sixpence each to 103 widows. Mr S. Shuffrey, as Trustee of Maddox's Charity, gave 30 pairs of boots. Clothing tickets came from the Trustees of Witney Charities, and gifts from Townsend's Charity.

WORKHOUSE CELEBRATIONS

The first treat of Christmas Day was the serving of coffee and tea for breakfast. For dinner there was roast beef, roast and boiled mutton, rabbits, plum pudding and beer. After dinner each man was given an ounce of tobacco, and each woman and non-smoking man had 2oz of tea and half a pound of sugar. Each inmate received an orange. There was cake for tea. Next day Dr Batt supplied the sick with mince pies and wine. Officers and inmates put on a concert in the evening.

WATCH THEFT

At Petty Sessions a 15-year-old girl was found guilty of stealing a watch worth 30/- from Mr F.S. Walters' jewellers' shop in Witney. She gave it to her mother, who pawned it for 3/6d. The mother received a sentence of one month's imprisonment, and the daughter was sent to a reformatory for two years.

1905

The Christmas message to Witney Gazette readers expressed contentment that most of the world seemed to be at peace, Russia being the great exception. Certainly, in that country nothing was going right. Strikes, uprisings, mutiny and government brutality all added to the suffering caused by the bloodthirsty war with Japan, which ended with Russian defeat in September.

In Parliament, a Women's Enfranchisement Bill was talked out amid laughter. This was not echoed by the Suffragettes, three of whom received short prison sentences in October. The Gazette's comments on the Bill were uncompromisingly negative.

Several motor accidents were reported, and one prosecution of a motorist for driving without rear lights, which delighted 'Jottings'. Drivers nationwide were becoming alarmed at the numerous laws which were being introduced to control their activities, and the zeal of the police in enforcing them. The Automobile Association was founded in June to protect the interests of motorists.

In Witney, shop assistants won the right to an adequate afternoon off on Tuesdays.

The Leys was now the official town recreation ground, and discussions were going on as to how it should be used. Vandals were spoiling the new amenity for others: what were the police doing about it? The question of Sunday sport and recreation was also troubling some people. Could exciting games and excursions be reconciled with the concept of Sunday as a day of rest?

There was more trouble with the water tower.

FIRE AT WITNEY MILL

Most of the factory hands had left when Mr. Gledhill the dyer discovered smoke issuing from the finishing room. He raised the alarm at 5.15pm and soon the whole town was aware of the fire by the prolonged whistle on the factory hooter. The Fire Brigade found that a large building, which faced on to Mill Street was on fire. The burning building was some 60 yards long by a width varying from 13 to 25 yards and having three floors. The ground floor contained an office and "gigs", altogether some dozen machines, comparatively new and of the latest construction. It was on this floor that the fire began, possibly through an overheated bearing. The first floor was occupied with the yarn store and whipping and blanket room, while the second floor was used as a spinning room with three pairs of machines and mules. Underneath the building ran the Windrush with a water-wheel. The Captain at once saw that it was useless to try and save any part of the building, as it was well alight and burning furiously. There was grave danger that the fire would spread to the Stock House and the engine house. On these two buildings the Brigade concentrated its efforts. The connection between the Stock House and the burning building was by a door on the first floor. The possibility of fire had been foreseen so the door and frame were of iron. The great heat soon buckled the iron door and the fight between the devouring element and the firemen was long and furious. In the engine room the fire did break in and there too, the work of the firemen was very hot.

About half an hour after the outbreak the roof fell with a great crash, and as the volume of flame increased it was thought expedient to telephone for assistance from Oxford. With commendable alacrity the City Brigade responded, and at 6.50 a steam engine fully manned, departed with four horses, with which they reached Witney in three quarters of an hour. An immense volume of water was then poured in from seven hoses and soon had the effect of suppressing the flames.

The fire could be seen from Bampton and Burford. Mill Street was soon packed with excited spectators, and locomotion became impossible. Happily Supt. Hawtin immediately wired to several constables in his division and soon had a strong force on the ground, which kept back the throng and allowed the firemen to move about freely.

By two o'clock the fire was all but out and the Oxford Brigade returned home. The Witney Brigade remained all night in case of a fresh outbreak. The Ambulance Corps connected with the Oxford Brigade arrived on bicycles, but happily their service was not needed.

According to the official report the estimated damage is £7,000.

WITNEY INSTITUTE TO BATH OR NOT TO BATH

At the A.G.M. of the Institute the Chairman suggested that the present time was a good one for bringing forward fresh proposals for the benefit of the Institute. The Hon. Sec. (Mr. Viner) said that there had been a suggestion that the old bagatelle room should be fitted up as a bathroom. Mr A. E. Horne thought the suggestion a good one provided a bath could be enjoyed by all for a nominal sum to members. Mr. Viner said the cost would be £20. The committee agreed to this proposal.

A JOLLY PEAL

The ringers from St. Mary's rang a muffled peal from 11.45 till 12 o'clock, then the mufflers being removed a joyous peal ushered in the new year. Mrs Jenkyn as usual honoured the ringers with her presence.

****

IMPROVEMENTS TO MILL STREET

The following letter has been received by the U.D.C.

Gentlemen,

Your council are doubtless aware of the awkward and dangerous corner in Mill Street near our Mill gates, and the present time *[after the fire]* offers an opportunity not likely to occur again for diverting and improving the course of the road at this point. Should your council think well to take this matter in hand, we are prepared to give the requisite ground in Rock House Close for a road not narrower than the present one, and to pay half the costs of the scheme, provided it can be carried through at the next April Quarter session; the old road being given us in exchange for the ground from Rock House Close.

We are, Gentlemen,
Yours faithfully
Chas Early & Co.

The Council felt that Messrs Early should pay all the cost. Mr Early replied that unless the Council paid half the cost (estimated cost £275) the work would not be carried out. Eventually it was agreed that the Council should do the work and pay £100 towards the costs, and Messrs Early to defray the remaining costs.

A further letter was received from Messrs Early withdrawing their offer. The Chairman said he was very sorry they had lost the opportunity to make such a great improvement.

SLEEPING ROUGH

At the police court before C. Early Esq., Thomas Phillips and Catherine Phillips were charged with sleeping in a shed in Stanton Harcourt on the 16th inst without having any visible means of subsistence, and were sentenced to 10 days imprisonment. On Monday before W. Smith Esq., John Cole of Newland was summoned for sleeping in a shed at Coggs, and was sentenced to 7 days hard labour.

R.D.C. IGNORES PIGS

The R.D.C. did well to ignore the complaint respecting the keeping of pigs within a certain distance of a dwelling house in Eynsham. It was proved that the pigsties were in a clean state and there can be no doubt whatever that when the by-laws were made, they were intended to be used only when filth reigned supreme. If all the by-laws of all the councils in the kingdom were carried out to the strict letter life would not be worth living. It is all very well to have these laws in hand, to put into execution when circumstances require it, but not at the promptings of some petty spite. How many farm houses .are there in the Rural District within 80 feet of a pigsty, doubtless hundreds, and yet no human being was ever injured by it.

THE CROFTS ROAD

Dear Sir,

Oh how can I appeal to the U.D.C., shall I appeal to the pathetic side? Can I take the Council with me at 5.30am (imagination only) on a wet winter's morn and ask them to listen to the slush slush slush of fathers sons and daughters as they tramp through the mud and water to their daily employment, and can I remind the Council that they have to stand in their boots for the next two hours then repeat the dose at breakfast time, or will the members come with me at 8.30am, and see the poor little children going to school not shod as well as they ought to be, some of them getting wet footed and having to sit in it at school. What wonder sir that when the attendance officer calls in a day or two to know how it is that John or Mary is not at school that the mother tells him the child has a cold. Or can the Council see the mothers going through the mud to do their daily shopping?

It is now some months since the owners of properties in the Crofts were called together to meet the committee. I believe 13 owners were present. Mr C. D. Batt in the chair said that the roads committee thought something should be done. The surveyor produced two estimates, one using foreign stone to make good the road and gutter, and curb the footpath, for £400, the other to use local stone for £150. It was agreed that the cheaper option should be carried out, and the owners pay two fifths of the cost and the Council the rest. That was a long time ago, and we have heard nothing since. Is it not about time that a Ratepayers Association was formed in the town that we may to some extent protect ourselves?

Yours truly
A. E. Horne

TEACHING TEACHERS TO TEACH TEACHERS

The Rector, in his speech to the school of Science and Art, complained of the small number of artisans who attended the very useful evening classes. Are the classes only to teach teachers who in their turn will teach other teachers? If this goes on year after year the general public will not be taught, and it is hard to see the purpose for which the classes exist.

COST OF EDUCATION

There can be no wonder at the expenditure on matters educational if the education secretary is to be allowed 1/- a mile to run his motor-car. If expenditure is generally on this scale there can be no wonder that it has reached 10d in the £. Doubtless there is a lot of money frittered away on what is called technical education. We have heard of many superficial subjects being taught. The latest to come to our attention is "washing". We are informed that in a certain village (Aston) not many miles from Witney the County Council actually pays a person to teach girls to wash linen. If anyone can point out a more wanton waste of public money I should like to know.

EARLY CLOSING

To the Editor

Dear Sir,

The proposal to shut the shops in Witney at 2pm on Tuesdays has been very favourably received by a large majority of the traders. There are some who object and one would have thought that when they found themselves in a minority of 12 to 1 they would have fallen into line with their fellows. This they have not done. There are occasions in life when we ought to make a sacrifice for the benefit of others. As far as Witney traders are concerned is not the present time one of these occasions?

Yours obediently,

FAIR PLAY

TRADERS SETTLE THEIR DIFFERENCES

We are glad to report that at a further meeting of the Witney Traders Society it was unanimously agreed to close at 1 o'clock on Tuesdays instead of three as heretofore.

Both the Witney Traders and their assistants are to be congratulated on the sensible conclusion that they have arrived at to close their shops at 1pm on Tuesdays. For some years assistants have had a so-called half-holiday once a week. First came the closing at 4pm on Tuesdays followed 2 years later by giving one more hour, still it was not a half-holiday. Recently assistants have been asking for another hour and the traders have boldly faced the matter by closing at 1 o'clock. We feel sure that everybody will do their best to make the half-holiday as valuable to the assistants as possible by shopping early. There are few people who have less time for recreation than shop assistants.

SELF HELP

Village life is proverbially monotonous; anything that can relieve that monotony should be welcome. Minster Lovell and Brize Norton have done something about it this winter. The first has established a troupe of niggers and the latter a dramatic society.

DEATH OF A WITNEY MAN

We regret to announce the death of Mr W. J. Clarke late master of the Witney Union Workhouse. Mr. Clarke was the last surviving member of a very old firm of coopers. More than half a century ago the deceased was a field trumpeter in the Oxfordshire Yeomanry, and a cricketer who in those days at times made his century. He enlisted in a Cavalry regiment, we believe the 9th Hussars, and saw a good deal of Foreign Service including the Indian Mutiny. Having got to the top of the tree as a non-commissioned officer, Mr Clarke retired, and was appointed relieving officer for Burford. Having served in that office for some years, he became master of the Witney Workhouse from which he retired 2 years ago.

THE ALIENS BILL

The Government have introduced the Aliens Bill, and it is sincerely hoped it will become law, or at any rate sufficient part of it to keep out of this country foreign criminals and other undesirables. Doubtless most of us still wish the country to be the home of the free, and would not like to put anything in the way of genuine able-bodied, honest immigrants landing on our shores, but the undesirables that have flocked to this country of late are so numerous that the time has arrived when some obstacle to the free introduction of this foreign evil should be applied.

****
****

EASTER SPORTS

The annual sports took place on Easter Monday in the presence of 4000 spectators. There were plentiful entries in all the events, but the competition was not sufficiently strong to produce any exciting finishes. The horse racing events were practically in the hands of three horses and these were so far superior to the others that they literally romped home.

WITNEY FOOTBALLER IN THE ENGLAND ELEVEN

The friends and admirers of Herbert Smith (and they are numerous) will be glad to hear that his play at Liverpool on Saturday last in the English team against Wales was such as to warrant the Selection Committee to include him in the England Eleven against Scotland at the Crystal Palace.

NAME CHANGE

An application has been made to change the name of the Public House in Curbridge now known as the Herd of Swine to the Lord Kitchener.

THE LEYS

The lease of the Leys recreation ground recently acquired by the U.D.C. is greatly appreciated by the inhabitants. Almost any evening a large number of towns people may be seen roaming about the spacious Leys enjoying the rural scene, watching the youngsters romping and the elders playing cricket. Seats have been provided in various parts of the ground, and this will be a boon to those who use the field. There can be little doubt that taking the Leys has been the most popular thing that the Council has done for many a year.

CRICKET IN OXFORD

Witney was well represented among the spectators at the Australian v Varsity match in Oxford this week. This was specially the case on Tuesday when the railway company issued cheap return fares by all trains. It is difficult to see why the company did not run a 'special' from Witney at say 1.30 on Tuesday seeing it is early closing day. One would have thought that it would have paid well, but the ways of the G.W.R. in business matters, are as we have remarked before, past finding out.

****

WOMEN'S ENFRANCHISEMENT

The Women's Enfranchisement Bill has been talked out of the House of Commons, and we do not suppose that there are many people even among the ladies themselves who regret its fate.

The Bill was one to allow women to vote at Parliamentary elections, and several politicians have taken up the matter declaring that the present law precluding women from voting is a great hardship. We do not believe it is anything of the kind. In the first place their domestic engagements absolutely prevent them from studying the numerous complicated questions that daily arise in the political world; and in the second place women with few exceptions, do not want a vote, indeed they would rather be without one. Then why bother them by thrusting upon them a responsibility they are naturally unfitted for or a privilege they do not want to possess.

THE DUST PROBLEM

It seems strange that the dust fiend, one of the present day evils, which causes incalculable amount of loss to millions of people, has not yet been successfully dealt with by an enlightened civilization. The rushing motorcar has increased this nuisance to an almost unbearable extent and we hear of people living near main roads having to leave their houses for this reason. The shopkeeper suffers to a serious extent but has to put up with damage to his goods as best he can.

WOMEN'S ENTERTAINMENT

The three societies that cater for the women of Witney – Young ladies' Social Guild, Girls' Friendly Society and Girls' circle are to combine to amuse not only themselves but their friends on Whit Monday. Tableaux, coon songs, and farce are some of the items, which are engaging the attention of their members.

CAR KILLS CHILD

Jessie Ward of Handborough was run over by a car belonging to Dr. Elsmore of Woodstock. The car stopped and Dr. Elsmore did all he could to help the child, who died the next morning.

The inquest heard from Frank Colley, a groom in the employ of Rev. W. Wilson of Handborough that there was a stall outside the 'Bell' and about 30 to 40 small children were throwing balls at bottles. "I heard a motor horn blowing several times and saw the car approaching. The children all stood clear. When the car was about 6 yards from the children the deceased tried to run across the road. She was knocked down and the front wheel ran over her." The occupants of the car, a small Humber registration AC 559, were Dr. Albert Charles Elsmore and his driver Charles Hollis. Jessie Ward, the daughter of John Ward, was five years old. John Ward said, "I knew she was up at the stall. She was with her sister aged 6 and another little girl. There was no one else in charge of the child."

*

The motor accident at Handborough, which resulted in the death of a child, has been declared by the Coroner's Jury to be purely an accident. Doubtless it was so and as motorcars run this one was going very slow indeed, but the question that arises is whether eight miles an hour along a crowded road is slow enough. It is a common thing for a horse and trap to walk through a crowd of that description and we see no earthly reason why a motor should go faster under certain conditions than a horse and trap, indeed it should go more slowly as the latter can pull up much more quickly and a horse will never run over a child if it can avoid it.

THE MANAGEMENT OF THE LEYS

At present the ground seems to be used as a promenade, more particularly on a Sunday, and a very proper use to make of it. But there seems to be the utter absence of anything like order in the place; boys pitch their wickets on the footpaths or anywhere they like, others take large stones onto the field, while others amuse themselves with making holes in the ground.

THE COUNCIL REACHES A DECISION ON THE CROFTS

Agreement could not be reached with the occupiers of properties in the Crofts and the Urban district Council. The Council has decided to proceed under the powers granted by the Private Streets Act of 1892, so that the street may be levelled, paved, metalled, flagged, channelled and made good, starting from a point 20 feet or thereabouts from the south-western corner of a house (No. 7) owned by Sarah Ann Steven and now empty, and thence running to an approximate distance of 600 feet in a southerly direction to the southern end of a house (No. 78) owned by John Williams and occupied by Edward Hawkes. The expense of such work to be apportioned upon the premises fronting and adjoining or abutting the road. The surveyor to prepare:

A, Specifications for the above work.
B, An estimate of probable expense of such work.
C, A provision of apportionment of the estimated cost.

WITNEY ANDOVERSFORD RAILWAY

The Light Railway Commission has authorised a railway of 24 miles from Witney in the East to Andoversford in the West giving railway facilities to Burford, Northleach and several villages on the route. Negotiations have started with Messrs Jackson & Co. contractors London, who have agreed to commence work as soon as bona fide offers have been received for £30,000 of the share capital and further to this they expressed willingness to run an engine to Northleach, some 15 miles, before any subscriber is called upon to fulfil his obligation to pay for the shares he has agreed to take.

The readers will upon reflection think this is a very reasonable and generous offer; it involves the raising of £30,000, an amount that should not be impossible to raise in this area.

PROPERTY SALE

Messers Habgood and Son offered for sale at the FLEECE HOTEL freehold property.
Lot 1: - a stone and brick built dwelling house with out-offices and garden known as Gloster Cottage in the occupation of F.T.French. The bidding started at £400 and was knocked down to Mr F.Berry for £520.
Lot 2: - a stone built and slated dwelling house No. 124 Corn Street in the occupation of Mr W. Long at a rental of £16 per annum, and purchased by Mr C. Talbot for £275.

******

TIMETABLE CHANGES

On and after July 1st a new train will leave Witney at 12.55 and the 11.06 will be discontinued. The alteration to the timetable will mean that the London morning mail will leave by the 10.14 instead of the 11.6, arriving in London an hour and forty minutes earlier than before. This should be useful to Witney traders, as it will allow them to get replies the next day. The 12.55 train will take letters which come in too late for the earlier train.

THE NEW WATER TANK

On Wednesday it was determined to fill the new tank. Mr Moore the engineer proceeded to pump all night. At about 8.50 the next morning Mrs Moore looking out from her bedroom window saw a small stream of water coming out of the east side of the tank and immediately afterwards she saw the side fly out with a great rush. The fall of water made a hole 3 feet deep, the water destroyed Mrs Moore's pretty garden. 45.000 gallons then flowed down Workhouse Hill.

The rate payers will be glad to hear that no loss will fall on their shoulders as a result of this unfortunate affair.

MONEY WASTED ON EDUCATION

Ever since what is popularly termed 'Whisky Money' has been handed to County Councils to spend on higher technical education there has been a scramble for it. Some of the claims may be legitimate but the utility of some is somewhat difficult to understand. There are the Horticulture, Farriery and cookery classes. Do our councillors really believe that a single horse

has been better shod, a dinner better cooked or a garden better tilled in consequence of lectures on these subjects? Then we believe there are lectures on hedging and ditching and even washing. Really, in connection with this matter one almost feels like saying "Teach your grand-mother to suck eggs".

THE RECREATION GROUND

It is early yet we suppose for the council to decide what is to be done in the way of games on the Leys. Cricket and football are played at present, but there is no provision for other games. It has been suggested that golf might be played there, but there is probably not enough room. We see no reason why there should not be some tennis courts. Surely there must be many people in Witney who would enjoy that most exhilarating pastime if they could find a court. The same remark applies to other outdoor games such as bowls.

SWIMMING

Scrutineer asks:
Who is responsible for the safety of bathers at the Witney Baths? If there is a committee does it ever meet? Whether the time has not arrived when the town authorities should have swimming baths under its control?

BAD ACCIDENT

Mr J. G. Ravenor and two friends were returning to Witney from Wantage, stopping off at the Railway Hotel in Oxford and then going on to the Automobile Club, which they left just after midnight. Near the South Lodge of Eynsham Park *(Barnards Gate)* they ran into the back of a conveyance belonging to Mr Pratley a coal dealer and bottle shooting gallery owner, who was returning with his shooting gallery having set it up for the day on Boars Hill. With Mr Pratley was his 18 year old daughter Mrs Smith. Dr Ravenor applied both brakes but a collision was inevitable. The force of the impact frightened the horse and it plunged forward pulling the forepart of the conveyance from the hind part. No one was much hurt but one of the party was struck by some of the paraphernalia sticking out behind the show cart and rendered insensible. The bonnet and both headlights of the car were smashed. Mrs Smith, who was much bruised, was placed on a conveyance and taken to her home 18 Corn Street, were she was attended by Dr Kelly. Six days later she gave birth to a child who died. Mrs Smith was later taken to the Infirmary were she died of internal injuries. Mr Ravenor was a careful driver and this was his first accident in 4 years of driving.

THE BATTLE OF THE BRIDEWELL

The F and I companies of Oxfordshire Volunteers had a field day on Saturday in the neighbourhood of North-Leigh. The idea was that a force was holding Bridewell farmhouse and premises, this consisted of the Bicester portion of F company under Lieut Cooper. The attacking party consisted of the Witney portion of F Company and the I company Oxford Cyclists' Corps, under the command of Capt. Darbyshire. Capt. Bennet acted as umpire. The attack started at about 4 o'clock and not withstanding the well sustained fire of the defenders, the enemy steadily advanced and after about $1^1/_2$ hours' engagement captured the place.

After the battle came refreshments, and it is doubtful if even the renowned cup that cheers but does not inebriate and the other fluids and brands so bountifully provided were more enjoyed than on this occasion. Altogether there were nearly 100 present and Mr, Mrs and Miss Gash and their staff of helpers were busily engaged in attending to the wants of their guests. After tea there was vocal and instrumental music, while the men enjoyed their pipes on the lawn.

AN EXCELLENT SEASON

Witney Rovers Football Club played 22 matches of which 16 were won, 2 lost and 4 drawn. 48 goals were scored for the club and 25 against.

THE VANDALS ARE ABOUT

Garden depredations are again the order of the day. We hear of fruit being stolen long before it is ripe as well as when it is in season. We would recommend those that suffer to make an example of the thieves by prosecuting them if they are old enough, and if they are not common sense will dictate the remedy to be applied.

GUARDIANS CRICKET MATCH

Witney vs. Chipping Norton Guardians

It was a pleasant sight to witness the middle aged (not to say aged) Guardians playing Cricket at Witney on Monday. More than usual interest was taken in the match as up to the present time each side has won 2 matches. The match started at 11.30 with the visitors batting first. At the end of the first innings Witney was ahead 116 to 114. In the second innings the superior bowling of the visitors told and they won a well played game. The weather being hot the cricketers got thirsty, and during the afternoon the unusual sight of a claret cup being taken onto the field was witnessed.

BANK HOLIDAY

The goods wharf and coal yard at Witney Station will be closed.

THE WAIL OF THE WITNEY WATER TANK

Oh pity me passer by!
You can, you will, you must-
I am the Witney Water Tank
That's lately been and bust.

Had they but taken proper care ,
And filled me with a spoon,
Although I must have bust one day
I'd not have bust so soon.

And now I hear (I must admit
The notion gives me pain)
There's going to be another try,
To fill me up again.

If this be so I only beg,
If there should be a spark
Of sympathy in any breast,
Don't do it in the dark.
Signed BARKINS

GAME LICENCE REFUSED

The clerk stated that James Buller of Ramsden had recently applied at Oxford for a game licence, and it was refused on account of his being a higgler, and he now applied to the Council for a licence. The application was refused on the same grounds as given in Oxford.

WHERE ARE THE POLICE?

The Leys are still being damaged. The damage done by mischievous boys and girls too, continues in our midst. In days gone by when the Witney Church Leys was practically a 'no man's land' the boys and girls amused themselves by pulling down stone by stone the wall of the Rectory ground. When the Leys was taken over by the Council for a recreation ground and the Rectory wall was repaired, we fondly imagined that the conversion of stone walls into fancy mounds in the grass would cease. It is not so, large 'toppers' have been removed and stones of various sizes are spread about the turf, some of them in a position to be dangerous to pedestrians walking from Corn Street to the Station.

Now this kind of depredation ought to be easily stopped. It all takes place in broad daylight, the police often perambulate the road, but how is it that they never or seldom detect the rascals? We hope our excellent Superintendent will not think it unnecessarily officious when we suggest that a little plain clothed detective work might lead to satisfactory results.

There is one other suggestion we would like to make. When boys are convicted of an offence of this kind a sound thrashing would we think prove a greater deterrent than fining the parents.

ACCIDENT AT THE MILL

A serious accident befell Flora Pitchet an employee at Messrs. Marriot's Mill on Saturday. In cleaning her loom her hand got caught in the machinery and was severely lacerated. She was promptly attended by Dr Kelly and was subsequently sent to the Radcliffe Infirmary where her thumb had to be amputated.

NEW TANK REFILLED

The new water tank which Messrs Young have been erecting during the past 5 weeks is finished with the exception of the roof. Filling began on Thursday 31st of August and by Friday the 1st September it was half full. The slow rate of filling is accounted for by the fact that it is only the surplus from the town supply that is being used for the filling.

VOLUNTEERS TO HAVE MEDICAL EXAMINATION

There has been much friction caused by the plan to medically examine all Volunteers. There has been much trouble many of the men objecting to the examination. In some cases where the officers had the tact to explain the matter and to request the men to undergo the ordeal, most of the men submitted, but in others where a highhanded policy was pursued some of the men have been dismissed for insubordination in refusing a medical examination.

This examination is being made to ascertain if the men are fit for foreign service and is naturally objected to by men who only volunteered to defend their country at home. The whole proceedings look very much as though the War Office means to abolish the Volunteers and to establish compulsory service. Now this is just what the English people will object to. To take the eldest son in every family away from his profession, business or employment for several years military service just at the period when he gains the knowledge essential to his career in life is so un-English and detrimental to the general welfare of the country that we doubt if it will ever be submitted to.

OTTER HUNTING

On Tuesday the Bucks Otter Hounds visited the district. Starting from Newbridge they worked up the Windrush to Ducklington, and then returned by the other stream to Hardwick. Unfortunately Mr Otter was not at home, and although the hounds worked remarkably well they were unable to find.

On Wednesday the meet was at old Shifford and some capital sport was enjoyed. The hounds got a good scent at 9.30 and it was not till 2 o'clock that the otter was killed near Mr Southby's plantation near Bampton. Some 200 ladies and gentlemen were present, all of whom took the keenest interest in the sport. The hunt were hospitably entertained by Mr F.D.Hurt of Bampton.

NARROW ROADS

Mr M.Florey drew the Council's attention to the narrowness of the District's roads. People were driven into the gutter on the sides of the roads in order to get out of the way of motors and he thought it was necessary that they should widen the District roads. Captain Wynter asked whether they were to pay for the convenience of the motorist. Mr Florey said the general public had to risk their lives for the motors, and he thought they should be protected. The Chairman said it was because the road-men did not cut the sidings wide enough. The Surveyor was instructed to see the sidings were properly cut away.

ELECTION OF BAILIFFS

A COURT moot of His Grace the Duke of Marlborough was held in the Town Hall. The Steward of the Manor, F. J. D. Westwell presided. The following were elected on the Jury:- Messers C. Viner, H. W. Springer, W. T. Felton, J. F. Marriot, W. Hammond, J. Verney, F. S. Walton, R. L. Eastbrook, A. E. Horne, J. Berry, F. Berry, W. G. Phillips and G. Owen.

The outgoing Bailiffs were Mr Viner and E. T. Leigh. The Jury elected Mr W. Smith jun and Mr J. E. Knight to be the new Bailiffs.

MOTOR BICYCLE ACCIDENT

As Mr T. Bradshaw was driving his motor bicycle with a trailer attached containing a friend, across Market Place on Saturday evening, he came in contact with a lad, who apparently did not attempt to get out of the way. The cyclist was going at a slow pace, so that the contact did not hurt him; his friend in the trailer was pitched out and sustained some bruises. Apparently the lad who caused the accident was not much hurt as he immediately quitted the scene.

LUNATICS COST RATEPAYERS MORE

Within the last few years there has been an increase of some 20% in the cost of Pauper Lunatics in this county, and during the last year the cost has increased from 8/9d to 9/11d per week. It is stated that there has been this large increase in the number of lunatics. Suppose the increase to be correct, why should the cost per head increase? Provisions were never cheaper and surely the greater the number in any establishment the cheaper it should be per head to keep them. A reason given for the increase is in consequence of the inspectors under the Lunacy Act insisting upon certain improvements. Apparently this department like that of the Local Government Board and other Government departments exists for the purpose of employing certain men to make all sorts of recommendations, utterly regardless of the cost to the ratepayer.

FREEMASONS MOVE

The Masonic Lodge has been removed from the Corn Exchange to the Church House, where a suitable room has been fitted up. The First Lodge Meeting was held there on Wednesday, and the members afterwards attended a dinner at the Fleece Hotel.

SUNDAY OBSERVANCE

At the Oxford Diocesan conference it was resolved that 'Worship and rest are the essential principles on which Christian observance of the Lord's Day should be based and subject to this as a safeguard of the religious observance of the day this conference is of the opinion that consideration is due to those who in the exercise of their Christian liberty, practice such forms of innocent recreation as does not deprive others of their rightful observance of the day'.

Already we see Golf Clubs have taken advantage of this resolution and decided to open their grounds on Sundays at 12.30. Why we wonder at that hour? Is it likely that people who are going to play golf at 12.30 will attend the morning service? Then caddies are not to be employed. One wonders how long a time that rule will be kept?

So far as we can gather the principal argument for Sunday amusement apologists is the effect that in the present day race for wealth and position many have not the time for proper recreation on the six weekdays, as we call Monday to Saturday.

The Sabbath was instituted as a day of rest. Can the excitement of motoring, golfing, croquet, cricket, football, racing, and railway excursions etc. be considered rest?

THE GAS WORKS

We understand that as a result of negotiations which have been going on for some time, a preliminary agreement has been signed for the sale of the works to a new company called the Mid Oxon Gas Company. We believe this will not involve any alteration in the management of the works.

POLICE COURT

C. Early Esq., on Monday fined Ellen Buckingham, said to be a nurse, 7/6d for being drunk at Newland, and sent Frank Reynolds, a tramp, to prison for 14 days hard labour for breaking a window in the Workhouse. Mr Finnis gave evidence in the latter case and P.C. Cox in the former.

BUTTER CROSS CLOCK

The clock was in darkness on several mornings this week even though the street lighting had not been extinguished.
Now as we understand it, one of the principal reasons for having the clock illuminated is that people on their way to work may be enabled to see the correct time. We feel sure it is only necessary to call the attention of the official, who ever he may be, to the fact that the clock is not illuminated for the matter to be righted.

A SUCCESFUL MUSIC CANDIDATE

Miss Annie Fowler, daughter of Mr Hariph Fowler, Springfield House, the Crofts, and former pupil of Miss Reynolds and Miss Davis, has been successful in gaining two first class certificates in Music in both practical and theoretical, at an examination held at the London College of Music.

ANXIOUS TO BE A HANGMAN

A large number of applications have been received at the Home Office for the vacancy as hangman caused by the death of Billington. The applicants hail from nearly all parts of the Country, but principally from the North. The hangman receives a retaining fee of £2-5-0 a week and is paid £5 and travelling expenses for every execution.

MISCHIEVOUS children in Witney should note the conviction of some youths in Tetbury for ringing street bells and otherwise annoying peaceable householders.

WITNEY PETTY SESSIONS

Ernest Peel of Pontriles Hereford, Gentleman was summoned for that he being the driver of a motorcar did fail to keep the lamp burning at the back of the car.

The Defendant did not appear.

P.S. Josey stated that on 18th inst at 7.40 he saw the defendant driving a motorcar without lights at the back. Witness stopped the car and the defendant said the light had just gone out. The lamp was cold.

Defendant was fined £1 with costs, and his licence was endorsed.

The prosecution of a motorist at Witney is a new departure and it is hoped that is a beginning of a new vigilant attention to this class of law breaking. It is hoped that the police will succeed in bringing to justice some of those reckless drivers who are continually driving to the common danger of His Majesty's subjects.

SMELLY GAS AGAIN

What is the matter with the Witney gas?

Some time ago we had complaints of Sulphuric odours coming from it at certain hours of the evening. Now the complaint is apparently of a Carbonic kind, for it is described as being the smell of a smoking lamp.

LADIES READING ROOM BOOM

A 'Book Tea' at the Ladies Reading Room was well attended on Tuesday, and much amusement was caused by guessing the title of the book that each person was dressed to represent. Some of the book symbols were very clever. A sum of £1 3s 9d was raised by the function.

HAPPY CHRISTMAS TO ALL OUR READERS

Once again Christmas is upon us, the time of Peace and Goodwill. For the first time this century we have a Christmas with no great war either in hand or in contemplation for all the nations of the earth appear to be at peace with each other. There is indeed nothing to mar the peace except the internal affairs of Russia, which may after all turn out to be the first steps in the regeneration of that unhappy country. As far as England is concerned most people are as prosperous and happy as in the nature of things can be expected. It is true that in the course of the next few weeks we will have a general election upon us, but that is no reason why we should not enjoy a peaceful Christmas.

We wish you all a happy Christmas

HAILEY PARISH COUNCIL MEETING

A meeting took place last week when there were present Mr. F. Habgood (chairman) Messrs F. B. Harris, T. Smith, H. Nutting, J. Harris and T. Harris.

On a proposition proposed by Mr. T. Harris and seconded by Mr. J. Harris. It was resolved to put the village pond in a reasonable state of repair. The Chairman and Mr. J. Harris were appointed a committee to carry out the work.

Messers. E. A. Blake, H. Nutting and G. T. Buckingham were appointed to distribute the charity bread at Christmas.

The Clerk Mr. Goatley was directed to write to the various owners of properties calling their attention to certain awkward and dangerous stiles.

RESIGNATION OF GOVERNMENT

MR BALFOUR TO SEE THE KING

LIBERAL CABINET TO BE FORMED

SIR H. CAMPBELL-BANNERMAN TO BE THE NEW PREMIER

NEW ELECTION TO TAKE PLACE NEXT MONTH

****

FATSTOCK SHOW AND SALE

Since the Christmas show and sale started 12 years ago this has been the most successful yet. The quantity and quality was the best ever.

Sale

On Thursday December 14th will commence a great **shilling sale** of Millinery, Drapery, Hosiery, Laces, Gloves, and corsets: also many novelties suitable as Xmas presents, hundreds of useful and fancy articles at the low price of 1s. each.

W. Hammond's High Street and West End.

1906

Liberal victory in the General Election in January brought Mid-Oxon a new Member of Parliament. Sir Henry Campbell-Bannerman continued as Prime Minister, having been appointed to take over from Mr Balfour in December 1905, when the question of tariff reform had caused turmoil in the Tory Party.

There was fine weather at Easter and a heat wave in the summer. Perhaps this is why sport is so prominent in this year's Witney Gazettes. A well-known Witney man played football for England, and his brother captained Oxford, both matches being won. Unfortunately, in their home town spectators at a local match caused serious offence by booing and hooting. The 'swimming baths' on the Windrush were smartened up, and an attendant was engaged to supervise the bathers. The existing Golf Club closed, but a new one was opened at Manor Farm, Cogges. There were suggestions for tennis courts and bowling greens to be set up on The Leys. Cycling was very popular: the Bicycle Gymkhana at the Parish Fete provided excitement and knockabout fun for the spectators.

Water was in the news during the drought. Levels were low, and consumers were warned that wasting water could be punished by law.

A 1904 petition from 1020 Temperance supporters doomed two of Witney's many public houses to closure. They were both respectable establishments, but both so close to other licenced premises that their sorrowing regulars could not claim that their absence led to serious hardship.

WITNEY GASWORKS:- COKE is now reduced to 4d per bushel. Special quotations for large quantities.

GREAT STORM

Serious damage was caused by one of the fiercest storms ever experienced here. Slates were sent flying, chimney pots displaced, sheds unroofed, fowl-houses blown over, ricks unthatched. At Mr Ransom's in the Market Place a window was blown into a bedroom, and at the Temperance Hotel the flagstaff bent down and got entangled with the telephone wires.

PIG CLUB SUPPER

Some 30 members sat down to their 4th anniversary supper at the Three Horseshoes. Mr A.E.Horne, Secretary, was pleased to announce a reserve fund of nearly £15 after compensation for losses had been paid. The contribution paid by members was a halfpenny per week per pig. The Chairman, Mr Smith of Corn Street, proposed a royal toast and another to 'Success to the Witney Pig Club'. He suggested that the Club should be re-named the Witney Pig Association in view of its success. He was in favour of more home-produced pork, to save the money paid out to foreigners for imported pigs. He saw no reason why Witney should not have a bacon factory like the one at Calne. The dinner ended with songs, Auld Lang Syne and the National Anthem.

SUICIDE TRAGEDY

The Coroner's Jury returned a verdict of strychnine poisoning, self-administered in a state of temporary insanity, on a 28-year-old man. The deceased had been receiving anonymous letters which may have caused him to be excitable and irritable. After a day of drinking with friends, he drank a solution of mouse poison bought from a local chemist.

ELECTION SPECIAL
1906

THE CANDIDATES

Candidates for Mid-Oxon in the General Election were the sitting M.P., Mr G. Herbert Morrell of Headington Hall, Oxford (Con), and Mr. E. N. Bennett of Hertford College, Oxford (Lib). One of the front rooms of the Corn Exchange was used by Mr. Bennett's Committee, while Mr. Morrell's Committee secured rooms nearly opposite the Wesleyan Schools. Canvassing was actively pursued, and literature of a 'more or less interesting nature' was widely circulated. The Liberal meeting at the Corn Exchange was the largest and most unanimous political meeting ever held in Witney.

POLLING DAY

Voting days varied according to area; in Witney polling took place on January 19th. Many local people had their first ride in a motor car on Polling Day, when prominent citizens lent their motors and carriages to the parties of their choice. Red ribbons for Liberals were prominent in the streets. The weather was fine. Mr. Bennett and Mr. Morrell both called into their Witney Committee rooms on their constituency tours.

LIBERAL LANDSLIDE

The final result for Mid-Oxon was:
BENNETT 4,585
MORRELL 4,144
Lib. majority 441.

State of Parties:
Lib 379, Con 157, Lab 51,
Nationalist 83.

NEW MEMBER'S DISTINGUISHED CAREER

Mr. E. N. Bennett, the newly-elected M.P. for Mid-Oxon, had a distinguished University career and has lectured at several Oxford colleges. His extensive travels include the exploration of the island of Sokotra (Indian Ocean) and a ride through Syria and Palestine. He was a war correspondent in the Cretan insurrection and the expedition to Khartoum. In the South African War he served in the Volunteer Ambulance Corps and commanded the Oxfordshire Volunteers in the Orange River Colony. He has written several books and prestigious magazine articles. Unmarried, he is a Guardian of the Poor for Oxford, and one of the most active supporters of Liberal politics in the area.

COMMENT

'The swing of the pendulum', 'the Education Act' and 'Chinese labour in South Africa' are all considered to be important factors in the downfall of the Conservative Party. In this part of the country we feel that the Education Act has dominated people's opinions. Honest citizens have been placed in the dock and had their goods seized for their conscientious objections to this unwanted Act. It outraged the good old English principle that representation must go with taxation, and it was antagonistic to that fair play which all Englishmen love.
Some uneasiness has been expressed in the daily papers at the success of the Labour candidates, who have achieved large majorities in several places. As they do not profess to belong to either political party, but simply to uphold the rights of the labourer, we do not share this concern. They are neither Socialists nor Anarchists, but are simply in Parliament to look after the interests of their class. Nothing but good can come to the Nation by having all classes directly represented in the Imperial Parliament.

NEW MEMBER'S MESSAGE

TO THE ELECTORS of the Mid-Division of the County of Oxford.

GENTLEMEN - I beg to offer my most sincere thanks to those of your number who enabled us on Friday last to win so signal a victory for the cause of Liberalism. You may rely on me to do my utmost in the House of Commons to promote the welfare of all my constituents, irrespective of their political opinions.

I am, Gentlemen, yours faithfully,
E. N. Bennett

Oxford, January 20th, 1906.

NEW STATION MASTER

Mr. H. Roberts has succeeded Mr R. G. Eaton as Station Master of Witney.

POLICE DINNER

Mr R. T. Ravenor presided at the annual dinner for the police of the area. During the evening songs were sung by Miss Hawtin, P.C. Hedges, P.C. Dorrell, P.C. Fisher and many of the gentlemen present. The Chairman proposed the health of the Police Force, paying special tribute to Supt. Hawtin's capability and efficiency. Three cheers were given for Mrs Hawtin and Miss Hawtin, and the Superintendent responded with many thanks.

HOUSE NUMBERS

One of the most useful things ever accomplished by the Witney Urban Council was the numbering of houses. The work was well carried out and proved to be a great convenience. Gradually, however, the numbers are disappearing, some painted out, and others illegible for want of cleaning. Is it not time house-holders were directed to comply with the requirements of the law and the local authority in this matter?

MID-OXON GAS COMPANY'S BILL

The Urban District Council Works Committee has studied the Bill in Parliament presented by the Mid-Oxon Gas Co., and has had a draft petition prepared against it.

Councillors were of the opinion that the Bill would seriously and adversely affect the Council and the ratepayers. Among the many points needing modification, the Bill appeared to threaten the Council's authority over the town's gas supply.

SLEEPING ROUGH

Four tramps, including a married couple, were convicted of sleeping rough at Stanton Harcourt. Two of the men were sentenced to 21 days' hard labour, and the couple to three months. Their five children were taken to the Workhouse at 5am; the Matron stated that they were in a filthy condition.

A PLEA

Newly-elected labour M.P.s are expected to work for the benefit of the working class. Is it too much to hope that the many M.P.s belonging to the legal profession will devote themselves to reforming the laws of the land, so that members of the public with normal intelligence can understand them?

ORCHESTRAL CONCERT

Witney Orchestral Concert Society played to a large and appreciative audience. The programme included Haydn's Surprise Symphony, the ballet music from Faust, and Entry of the Gladiators. Miss Jannett Hayward's songs gained encores, and Mr. D. R. Macdonald's flute solos proved him to be an artist of high merit.

THE CHURCH IN CENTRAL AFRICA

The Bishop of Licoma came to Witney in connection with the Universities' Mission to Central Africa. He told the meeting that the Licoma Lake diocese was now fully organised, with 22 clergy, including four natives, white staff between 40 and 50, between 2000 and 3000 communicants, and 13,000 children in their schools. The work on the Cathedral had all been done by native Christians, even including women and children.

FOOTBALL SUCCESS

Mr. Herbert Smith of Witney, skipper of Reading, was selected to play for England against Ireland. England won 5-0. Remarkably, Mr. Smith's brother captained the Oxford team on the same day, when the score was 5-1 to Oxford. Why should Witney not have its own team? There is plenty of talent and plenty of time, and lots of people in this neighbourhood who love to witness a good match.

CONFIRMATION

The Bishop of Oxford conducted a Confirmation Service in the Parish Church before a large congregation.

DEATH: February 24th, at the 'Grey House', Filkins, the Rev. Canon Norris (formerly Rector of Witney) aged 81 years.

SAD EVENTS

'The King of Terrors', as death has been, sometimes erroneously, called, has been busy during the past week; among his victims is the Rev Canon Norris, who for a quarter of a century was Rector of Witney. It is no easy matter for the Rector of a place like Witney to so carry out the duties of his high office, for any length of time, without giving offence to somebody. Yet Canon Norris succeeded, for we do not believe he left behind him a single enemy. On the other hand his kindly manner and upright dealing with his parishioners, gained him a host of friends both from within and without the Church's circle. We are quite sure we are voicing the feelings of his late parishioners when we express regret for the loss of so good a man as Canon Norris.

The deaths are also announced this month of Mrs Charlotte Early, aged 83, widow of Mr Richard Early; Mrs Rachel Clinch, 86, widow of Mr James Clinch, and Mrs Hannah Brantom, 70, wife of the Rev J. Brantom.

BOGUS DRAPERS

Strange travelling drapers are calling at houses and persuading housewives to order calico, flannel, towels etc at ridiculously low prices. The traveller then produces a piece of material which the lady buys on the spot. Unfortunately the calico, flannel and towels she has paid for never arrive.

WITNEY RECREATION GROUND

The Committee of the Recreation Ground are contemplating the formation of GOLF LINKS, TENNIS and BOWLING LAWNS. Any person desirous of joining clubs for playing on either, should communicate with either F.M. Green or J. Knight.

COMMENT: We feel sure that many residents of Blanketopolis will avail themselves of the healthgiving games proposed. The golf links at Northfield Farm will not exist after the present season, so the provision of a course (however small) would be welcomed by experienced and new players alike. The game of bowls is becoming more and more popular for men of all ages. Tennis will appeal to many of the younger inhabitants. Billiards, chess and cards are all very well in moderation, but these outdoor pastimes are much more desirable in suitable weather.

A REFRACTORY PAUPER

At the Police Court an inmate of Witney Workhouse was charged with refractory conduct. This man had left the Workhouse with his wife and two children, and succeeded in getting several donations on the pretext of becoming a reformed character. He immediately got drunk, returned to the Workhouse and created a disturbance, He was sentenced to ten days' hard labour.

FIRE AT WITNEY MILL

At 4am on March 22nd, night workers at Witney Mill discovered the roof of a detached building was on fire. The Engineer at the Water Tower was instantly notified, and started the pumps to ensure a good supply of water to the Witney Mill Fire Brigade, who soon extinguished the flames. Damage is estimated at £300 or £400.

INNS MAY CLOSE

In 1904 1020 Witney inhabitants signed a petition with regard to the number of licenced houses in the town; Temperance supporters felt that one per 106 persons was excessive. The brewers were asked to come to some arrangement, but failed to do so. At last month's Brewster Sessions, the cases for and against closure of the Jolly Tuckers in West End, and the Malt Shovel, in Corn Street, were examined.

Both houses are small, clean and well-kept, and do a good trade in beer, stout and mineral waters. There was no complaint against either, but their nearness to other licenced premises meant that closure would not cause hardship to the public.

Both houses were granted provisional licences, but were referred to the Compensation Authority at Oxford, which provides compensation for houses obliged to close.

****

CANINE PESTS

The dog nuisance in Witney is becoming almost unbearable. The number of animals constantly prowling about are not only a source of considerable danger to cyclists, but also to pedestrians; recently within the short space of a week no less than three persons have been knocked down by large dogs rushing against them. There is apparently no remedy for the unfortunate sufferers unless the dog should bite.

WORKHOUSE FATALITY

A woman of 87 who suffered from mental problems fell out of an upstairs window of the Workhouse, and was killed instantaneously. The Coroner heard evidence that she had lived in Filkins but no longer had a home there; it is thought that she might have been trying to go back there when she left her bed, opened the window and fell out while the attendant was absent on her rounds.

HEALTHY WITNEY

The Medical Officer's report on the health of the town of Witney is very satisfactory. Infectious diseases are practically unknown, and the infant mortality rate is considerably less than half that of the country generally. It is evident that people who are anxious that their babies should live (and who are not?) should take up their residence in the locality.

****

GAMES FOR THE LEYS

The idea of golf on the Leys has been abandoned, as the Committee has been advised that the field is not suitable. The idea has been expressed that tennis and golf were games for the upper classes, and that any enclosure would exclude the general public. The Committee assures doubters that nobody is to be excluded, and that the ideas of golf and tennis came from working class men.

PLENTY OF VEAL

A cow belonging to Mr T.F. Gardner, of West End, Witney, gave birth to three calves. The family are all alive and doing well.

LATE RECTOR'S ESTATE

The Rev Canon Norris left estate of the gross value of £6,283.

EASTER MONDAY

The weather was glorious on the public holiday. Many visitors came to Witney, and the annual sports were attended by 4000 people, a record number. The one drawback was the dust raised by numerous motor cars; the streets were not watered as the men were on holiday. Even on country roads nowadays cyclists and pedestrians have to suffer clouds of dust. How long will the public tolerate this state of things?

HAPPY FIELD DAY

On Easter Monday about 30 Boys Brigade members joined other local companies for a Field Day in Oxford. After a short parade at the Wesley Memorial Church, the boys marched up the hot, dusty hill to Cumnor, where they picnicked and drank vast quantities of mineral water. Football followed, and then they marched back to tea at the New Road Baptist Schools. After a walk round the City there was an informal 'sing-song', the genial Chairman's solos being the most popular.

LADY M.P's?

Ladies in the gallery set aside for them caused a hysterical scene in the House of Commons when Women's Suffrage was debated. In spite of this, we see no reason why women who are householders and paying rates and taxes should not vote at parliamentary elections. However, this would certainly not mean that they would be entitled to stand for election as members. This week's disgraceful exhibition shows that it would never do to have the ladies sitting as members of the House of Commons.

POPULAR BRIDE

The wedding has taken place of Miss Elsie Maria Early, elder daughter of Mr and Mrs Charles Early of 'Woodlands', to Mr Ferrand Edward Corley. The bride is well-known in Witney for her charming manner sympathetic kindness and extensive work for charity. We wish the couple long life and happiness in their new home in far-off India, where Mr Corley has an appointment as professor of History and English at the Christian College, Madras.

BATHING PLACE

What is to become of the Witney Bathing Place? Formerly there was a committee to look after it, but we believe at the present moment that committee never meets, and it is getting into a disreputable state. Could not the Council acquire the concern, so that it might be put into decent order? A bathing place, where children can be taught to swim, is an absolute necessity, and should be provided in every town.

PARENTS FINED

Two Leafield couples were summoned for allowing their children to go out while suffering from Scarlet Fever. Each parent was fined 10s.

FIRE TRAGEDY

A 66-year-old farmer of Minster Lovell has died of burns received at his home when his bed burst into flames. He had just lit a candle, and the bedclothes and curtains round the bed somehow caught fire. His wife managed to escape.

YOUNG PESTS

Many residents with houses facing the principal streets are much annoyed at having chalk marks put on the doors and walls of their houses, and then this kind of amusement is varied by the ringing of front door bells. Surely in these days of education, people have a right to have their homes protected from this kind of annoyance.

LIBERAL SMOKER

Our new M.P., Mr. E. N. Bennett, was guest of honour at the smoking concert given by the Witney Liberal Association at the Corn Exchange. He received a hearty welcome. In his acclaimed speech he expressed warm thanks to his Witney supporters, and gave some amusing comments on his first days in Parliament. He spoke briefly of the Trade Unions' Disputes Bill and the Budget.

Songs which entertained the audience included 'The Pleasant Month of May' and 'Old King Cole', both by the Magdalen Glee Singers, and 'Take a Pair of Sparkling Eyes' by Mr. C. Child.

*

A COTTAGE TO LET, No 22, The Terrace, Gloucester Place. Apply T. Andrews, No 53, High Street.

*

PROMENADE CONCERT

An alfresco entertainment was given in Messrs Marriott's field by the Witney Temperance Band and others. The programme consisted of several selections by the Band, a comic cricket match by men in fancy costumes, a comic song and a laughable sketch. There was a large attendance to enjoy the fun provided.

PERAMBULATOR MENACE

Frequently two or even three juvenile carriages abreast are to be seen on the pavement, causing pedestrians to take to the road. We believe there is a bye law forbidding this. Someone should see that it is enforced.

******

TAVERNS TO CLOSE

The County Licensing Committee has decided that the Jolly Tucker in West End and the Malt Shovel in Corn Street must close, as many residents have signed a petition claiming that there are too many licensed houses for a town the size of Witney. Claims must be submitted by the owners to the Compensation Authority before June 30.

AN UNUSUAL PREACHER

The converted collier Mr Moses Welsby ('Owd Mo') has visited Witney to preach at the Wesleyan Chapel, address the Men's Bible Class and deliver a lecture on 'Twenty Years with Thomas Champness'. All the events were well attended.

WITNEY SWIMMING BATHS

A PUBLIC MEETING will be held in the TOWN HALL, on WEDNESDAY [June 6] NEXT, at 8pm, when all interested in bathing are invited to attend.
H. SHUFFREY, Hon. Sec.

WANTED,
 an **ATTENDANT** for the above. Apply before 6pm on Wednesday, June 13th next to H. SHUFFREY, 29, Church Green.

LIBERAL FETE

A crowd of 3000 attended the Whit Monday fete. For the cycle parade only five riders turned up in fancy costumes. Mr. Whitcher as the 'Mikado' looked very good, and the Misses Eaton wore pretty Japanese costumes. The Witney Band led the procession to the cricket ground. Professor Wishart, the conjuror and escapologist, gave a novel entertainment. A tug-of-war between married and single was easily won by the married. In the Ladies v. Gentlemen cricket match, with the Gentlemen batting with sticks, the Ladies won by a comfortable eight wickets. The evening was taken up by political speeches, including one by Mr. Bennett M.P.

BATHS MEETING

At a sparsely attended meeting, a new committee was voted in, and it was resolved that the Urban Council be asked to provide proper Swimming Bath accommodation for the town at the earliest possible moment.

To the Editor, Witney Gazette:
Sir - Will you kindly allow me a little space in your paper for a word about the Baths. I wish to ask the ladies and public generally to kindly patronise them. I may say the place has been thoroughly scrubbed and disinfected. Notices have been put up, forbidding writing or scribbling on the boards of the baths. Every attention will be given to bathers; my desire being to get the affair in a good and sound condition financially, and at the same time to provide a good and sound bathing place.
I remain yours faithfully,
FRED SMITH, Attendant.

CHRISTIAN SOCIALISM

At the Wesleyan Chapel the Rev. Mark Guy Pearse spoke movingly of 'Christian Socialism, or Stories of Work in West London'. He described the dreadful conditions of London's poor, and pleaded for less selfishness and more sympathy from the Church. The election of Labour members of the House of Commons gave him great hope: he would like to see them in the House of Lords as well.

PORTSMOUTH REVISITED

The Witney Annual Trip will be to Portsmouth this year.

FAREWELL MEETING

Mr. and Mrs. Corley are about to depart for India. At the Men's Bible Class they received many good wishes, and Mrs Corley (the former Miss Elsie Early) was thanked sincerely for all her work and support for the class.

A WITNEY WATERLOO HERO

The tombstone of Sergeant Major Patrick Moulder, a native of Witney, stands in the Churchyard opposite the Almshouses. He spent 15 years in the 15th or King's Regiment of Hussars, and fought at Waterloo. In 1817 he joined the Oxfordshire Yeomanry as Regimental Sergeant Major, continuing until his death in 1838, aged 51. To commemorate the anniversary of Waterloo, Mr. F. M. Green has had the tombstone cleaned and renovated.

MODERN LANGUAGES - Miss Rust, retiring from the Grammar School, purposes, if possible, to remain in the District to give Private Tuition in the above. For particulars apply to Miss Rust, The Grammar School, Witney.

WANTED by a girl of 16, a situation as UNDER-HOUSEMAID or kitchen-maid. Apply F., Witney Gazette.

INSPECTOR REQUIRED

The Witney Rural District Council is advertising for an Inspector of Nuisances, including the Scavenging of four parishes. The District comprises an area of about 73,780 acres and has a population of about 15,877. The salary will be £120 per annum inclusive of all travelling expenses. Security in the sum of £100 will be required.

DR BARNARDO'S HOMES

A House-to-house collection, made on behalf of the above homes, amounted to £6.8s.6½. This sum was duly forwarded, and a letter thankfully acknowledging the receipt of the money has been received.

GOLF MEETING

At a meeting of those interested in golf, a proposition that the Witney Golf Club be resuscitated was carried, and a Committee was formed to place a scheme before a second meeting.

FOUND - A PIGEON; owner can have same by paying expenses. S. Mills, Asthalleigh.

COUNCIL LECTURES CRITICISED

At the annual meeting of the Church Day and Sunday school teachers, the delegates discussed the question of what became of their scholars after they left school. The evening classes provided by the County Council were criticised for being irrelevant to the scholars' lives. In mathematics, hard sums were taught which would be forgotten by the next week. The cookery teachers demonstrated with utensils and equipment never available to country cottage dwellers. The teachers agreed that Reading Rooms should be provided in every village at the Council's expense.

ARTIST IN TROUBLE

A tramp describing himself as an artist went to the Fleece Hotel and asked to make a drawing of the house, but the landlord ejected him because he was very drunk and using bad language. He pleaded guilty in court and was sentenced to seven days' imprisonment.

NEW SMOKING LAWS?

A House of Lords Committee suggests that smoking by children under 16 should be made illegal, and anyone selling cigarettes to children should be fined. In our opinion these drastic proposals are none too severe. The smoking boy is, as a rule, far inferior in both body and brain when he arrives at manhood to those who have abstained from the pernicious habit. As to adult smoking, opinions differ. It is generally admitted that no great harm follows the use of tobacco by adult persons. On the other hand, the soothing influence of the weed to the weary body and mind is well known and appreciated by a very large number of the adult population of the world.

TRAGIC FAMILY

In May we recorded the death of a Minster Lovell farmer when his bed caught fire. The family's story since then shows that 'facts are stranger than fiction'. The son who saved his mother from the blaze quarrelled with his married sister over money matters, and the mother left the home. The son married, and appeared to be happy, but three weeks later he attempted to shoot his sister. Failing, he turned the gun upon himself. The verdict at the inquest was 'suicide while temporarily insane'.

A FOWL CASE

A father and son of Eynsham were found guilty of stealing two fowls, value 3s, from Mr John Pimm's orchard. A witness described hearing a shot and seeing the younger man pick up two birds; the accuseds' story that they had shot a thrush and later failed to find it was not accepted. They were fined £1 or 14 days in prison: the elder defendant refused to pay and was removed in custody.

PARISH FETE

Superb weather greeted the fete in the Rectory grounds. Among the novel, varied and up-to-date attractions was a decorated cycle parade. Miss Moore of the Water Tower gained first prize with her beautiful representation of a swan. 76 daintily dressed children of Saint Mary's Schools then sang and danced delightfully in the Old English Revels. After tea came the Bicycle Gymkhana. Races included obstacle, tilting at the ring, potato and bucket and egg and ladle. The costume race, in which contestants had to ride round the ring, dismount and don a more or less picturesque garb, elicited roars of laughter. Clock golf, the prize-giving and an enjoyable evening dance on the Rectory lawn completed a happy and successful day.

FOR SALE - New Victor GRAMOPHONE; exhibition sound box; flower horn, records; cost £6, would exchange with part cash, for good cycle. Can be heard at 90, Corn Street, Witney.

IMPERFECT ROAD REPAIRS

The Market Place at Witney has for some weeks been under repair, and apparently the work done has not reached perfection. The fact is the money spent thereon will be entirely wasted unless the heavy traffic is diverted therefrom. There is no reason why posts or rails should not be placed on the West side, leaving a road way at the top, bottom and East side. It is pretty certain that unless something of this kind is done the market will some day have to be shifted, for the ratepayers cannot be expected to be continually spending large sums of money on this alone.

WITNEY DEANERY MISSIONARY ASSOCIATION

At the annual festival of the above Association the Bishop for the Gold Coast was a prominent speaker. He stressed that improvements in the intelligence and behaviour of natives of the Lagos colony were not achieved because of 'civilisation' but in spite of it, as drink in the form of millions of gallons of the vilest German gin was being imported into West Africa. It was the efforts of the Christian missions that had brought about the changes for the better; more chaplains were desperately needed to continue their work.

WATER WASTAGE

There is concern in the U.D.C. about water consumption, especially at night, in this period of drought. The well from which our supply comes is 10 feet below its usual level. The Council is appealing for economy, and considering the use of meters in all cases where public water is used for gardens. Consumers are reminded that wasting water is a criminal offence, which can be severely punished.

TERRIBLE ACCIDENT

Mr and Mrs Leeming were cycling from Buckingham to Ducklington to visit relatives, and had passed through Eynsham when Mrs Leeming's machine swerved into the path of a butcher's cart. She received serious head injuries and, in spite of the efforts of a lady cyclist and a motorist who drove to fetch the Eynsham doctor, she died in a trap in which she was being conveyed to Ducklington. At the inquest fatigue, heat exhaustion or her dress catching in the wheel were suggested as causes for Mrs Leeming's swerve, and the verdict was Accidental Death.

SHADE NEEDED

During the exceptionally fine weather The Leys have been a paradise for children. We suggest that the planting of trees to give more shade would improve our recreation ground still further, and if some philanthropist - a Witneyite living abroad, perhaps - would provide some seats, many old Witney people would be most grateful.

FIRE BRIGADE OUTING

Members of Witney Fire Brigade were invited by Captain Smith and Lieutenant Early to a picnic at Bablockhythe. Among the activities they enjoyed were a scratch cricket match, a substantial tea, quoits, and various games, boating and fishing. After their exertions they sat down to supper, after which Captain Smith distributed the prizes won by the men at the previous week's competition.

GREAT HEAT

The temperature on September 1 was probably a record for that date. Shade temperatures were: 9am 78, 1pm 89, 3pm 91, 5pm 88, 9pm 79. Mean temperature for the 12 hours was 85.

THE FAIR - GOOD AND BAD

Messrs Taylor, Thurston & Ball's exhibitions have never been better than they were this year, being excellent and free from vulgarity. However, the conduct of some attending the Fair was not so orderly as it should have been, to say the least. Squirts, confetti etc are rightly banned, but some people saw fit to throw flour and even blue bags at innocent passers-by, annoying them and spoiling their clothes. One person was even robbed of some ornaments she was wearing while being powdered by 2 or 3 youths.

MOTORING PERIL

As though there were not enough ills already attendant upon motoring, Sir James Crichton-Browne, a doctor of no mean reputation, has found yet another evil, not for the public to tolerate, but one which affects the motorist himself. Sir James says the rushing along the roads by the motorist has a similar effect upon his brain as the bolting of one's food has upon one's stomach. Insanity, he says, is the inevitable goal towards which a large number of motorists are rushing.

WATER SHORTAGE

There is much concern on the Council about the water supply. Notices have been issued on the use of water for gardening, but the leakage at night continues. Until the new valves which have been ordered arrive, it is impossible to trace the leak.

CHORAL SOCIETY

The new Witney Choral Society is rehearsing Haydn's 'The Creation', S. Coleridge Taylor's 'Hiawatha's Wedding Feast', 'The Miller's Wooing' by Eaton Fanning and 'When Hands Meet' by Pinsuti.

NEW GOLF CLUB

A site on Mr. Mawle's farm has been recommended as the new golf course. Capital outlay would be about £50, annual expenditure about £75. Entrance fee £1 1s, annual subscription £2 2s, ladies £1 1s; out of town members: gentlemen £1 1s, ladies 10/6.

DEATH OF MRS EARLY

We regret to record the death of Mrs Sarah Early, wife of Mr Charles Early, at the age of 82. Mr and Mrs Early were probably the oldest couple in Witney, having married in June 1848. A staunch Methodist, she had 3 children, 12 grandchildren and many friends. She was a generous giver, often anonymous, to various charities.

LANDLORD ASSAULTED

A labourer of no fixed abode was fined £1 on each of two charges, one of assault and the other of malicious damage to the extent of 2 shillings. He had used bad language in the bar of the Angel Inn, and when told to leave he refused, struck the landlord several times, and kicked in a window.

BEWARE OF THORNS

Council hedge cutting will soon be in full swing, with its accompanying hazard to cyclists of thorns scattered in the road. Cycling, probably the most useful invention of the nineteenth century, is used by tens of thousands of men (and women) from Peer to Peasant, for both business and pleasure. A little care exercised by the hedge-cutter would save a deal of trouble.

BALLOON RACE

The winning balloon in the International Balloon Race, 'The United States' (Lieutenant Lahn), passed over Stanton Harcourt at 7am on October 1st. It was flying so low that the trail ropes touched the trees and even the earth. The occupants asked some residents questions as to the village, county and even distance to the sea. Then the balloon rose rapidly to a great height and was soon lost to view.

TEMPERANCE REFORM

At a meeting in the Marlborough Lane Meeting Hall the Rector (Rev. J.R. Kirby) suggested that temperance reform had been retarded by two causes: extremists who went for all or nothing, and the fact that drunkenness was regarded by some as a subject for laughter and song rather than for profound sorrow. Mr. Cowley, of London, blamed the removal by Mr. Gladstone of the light wine duties for the great increase in drunkenness among women.

DEATH OF FORMER M.P.

Mr. G. H. Morrell, our Member of Parliament until recently, has died in Germany rather suddenly; the heart trouble and dropsy from which he suffered had seemed to be improving. He was held in the highest esteem by both supporters and opponents, and had a distinguished career in natural science, sport and the Law as well as in politics. He was a generous donor to many philanthropic institutions. A special train from Oxford conveyed a large number of mourners from all parts of the country to his funeral at Streatley.

DRESS MAKING - APPRENTICES WANTED; High Class Work. G. O. Tite, Waterloo House, Witney.

RIFLE CLUBS

The Duke of Norfolk is strongly recommending Rifle Clubs as a winter evening pursuit. He writes: 'I should like to bring very forcibly to the notice of all Englishmen how incumbent it is upon them that they should become skilled in the handling of a weapon, which can be used in defence of their country should ever they be called upon to defend its shores.'
Witney's 'F' Company of Volunteers showed their shooting prowess when they competed for over 30 prizes at their annual competition. Many local businesses and individuals donated prizes or money for the prize fund.

OFFENSIVE FOOTBALL SPECTATORS

A supporter of the Burford team which played Witney Centrals recently complains of the booing and hooting by spectators which spoilt his enjoyment of an otherwise pleasant match. It is not only in Witney that this happens. Young men should cultivate the valuable quality of self-control. Football is certainly far and away the best winter game yet invented, and it would be nothing short of a calamity if the rowdy conduct of the spectators should ever cause the sport to be banned by all self-respecting citizens. Fortunately cricket does not suffer from such tasteless behaviour.

WALNUT THIEVES

At Petty Sessions two Eynsham men were fined 16/- each for stealing walnuts worth one penny from Mr J.G. Pimm's orchard. Three boys were birched for the theft of walnuts worth 3d from an orchard belonging to Mr Banting.

THE CROFTS DECISION

At a special sitting of the Witney Bench the Magistrates decided that The Crofts should be made up at a cost of £483 5s 4d, the Council to contribute one fourth and the house owners the rest. It is a welcome decision after many years of legal wrangling.

DISTINGUISHED CLERGYMAN'S DEATH

The Rev. W.O. Jenkyn has died, aged 84 years, at Oriel House, Witney. In addition to regular Church duties, he was Chaplain to Lord Nelson in 1850, and in 1859 he became assistant Chaplain at the English Church at St. Petersburg. He returned from Russia in 1864. As Vicar of East Garston, Berks, he organised Church restoration and relief for parishioners made homeless by several disastrous fires. He had many friends in Witney, where he took up residence in 1901.

LEAKAGE FOUND

The Surveyor reported to the U.D.C. that he had found out that water was leaking from two broken service pipes near the Blanket Hall. He had replaced the pipes, and the result was the saving of two hours' pumping daily. His exertions were commended by several Council members.

SOCIALISM

One of the Labour parties has insisted that its representatives shall pledge themselves to the Socialist ticket; indeed, there is a growing number of persons who believe this creed is the only remedy for the evils they have to contend with. Taking from the man who has capital and distributing it among those who have not is, of course, downright robbery and immoral to the highest degree. A strong sense of right and wrong keeps English people from embracing Socialism so long as they are not driven to it, but there are very disquieting signs that the heartless conduct of some capitalists may entirely change the principles of many persons. The tyranny of American tinned meat packing employers has recently been exposed in 'The Jungle' [by Upton Sinclair, published 1906], but we do not have to go to the United States to find examples of employers who pay starvation rates and refuse to help their workmen in cases of disablement and sickness. Rich noblemen, too, have discharged long-serving workers who have then embraced Socialism.

The probability is that Socialism, if ever established in this country, will have been produced by the short-sightedness and selfishness of the men who have the most to lose by it. Let us all be wise in time. "Live and let live" is an old saying, and a very good motto for us all.

CHRYSANTHEMUM SHOW

The Committee's plucky decision to hold an exhibition in spite of last year's adverse balance was rewarded by a large attendance and an excellent show. Many prizes were earned for chrysanthemums, primulas, fruit, vegetables and needlework. Witney's Quadrille Band played at intervals, and the evening promenade concert of pianoforte and song was much enjoyed.

A SERIOUS CASE

Two Handborough men were found guilty of setting fire to two stacks of straw valued at about £60. The men had spent Guy Fawke's Day drinking, and left the public house saying they were going to have a bonfire. The Court did not believe their story that they had gone to the rickyard to get some straw to start the bonfire, but that a match carelessly thrown away when one of them lit his pipe had caused the ricks to catch fire. They were sentenced to 4 months' hard labour.

WITNEY STREETS

To the Editor of the Witney Gazette:

Sir, - Has the time arrived when it has become very nearly obligatory on us as townsfolk to look into the matter of the behaviour of the young men and women of the town?

Walk down any of our streets after dark, and the jostling and horse-play of the men and boys, and the equally objectionable "fun" of the other sex, is becoming a by-word and reproach to us. This leads me to a perhaps more important phase of the matter, and this is the slackness of the parents in allowing (in some cases) quite young children to run the streets until a late hour. I was taught when a child it was "Early to bed, early to rise, makes a man healthy, wealthy and wise", but we in Witney at least have improved on this, and I am afraid not for the better.

Yours truly,

H.J. Fidler,
14 West End

PRESENTATION TO MR. HERBERT SMITH

After the football match at Reading on November 10 Mr. Herbert Smith was the recipient of some valuable wedding presents from the Reading Football Club, which he has captained for the last 7 years. A well-subscribed fund produced a solid silver salver, a cabinet of silver plate and cutlery, and a very handsome bracelet for his fiancée.

MARRIAGE: Smith-Lawton November 19th. at Holy Trinity Church, Matlock Bath, Derbyshire, by the Rev. J. W. Marsh, assisted by the Rev. Charles Baker (vicar), Herbert Smith, of Witney, to Jessie Lawton, of Matlock Bath.

NSPCC

At a meeting held in Witney in connection with the NSPCC, Miss England spoke about the Society's methods, and revealed that during the past year ten houses in Witney had been visited by the Inspector, because of concern for the welfare of 32 children. Three cases came under the heading of ill-treatment, five of neglect and two of evil surroundings. The Inspector had visited the town 23 times and made 102 supervisory visits to the children, who were in their own homes but under the care of the Society. Prosecution, she stressed, was only used as a last resort.

GOLF CLUB OPENED

The new Witney Golf Club was inaugurated with a closely-fought contest between Sherlock and Cowley, two well-known professionals. The match was played over the whole day, Sherlock eventually emerging the winner. The 9-hole course at Manor Farm, Coggs, has attracted a large number of members, some from Oxford.

WHAT IS CRUELTY?

What humbugs we English people are. Here we have a Society for the prevention of cruelty to animals supported by everybody in the land, and if a horse is worked while lame or with a bit of its skin rubbed off, the owner is promptly hauled up before the Magistrates, and fined, and properly so. Yet a deer may be taken from a herd, peacefully browsing in a park, like a flock of sheep, and be hunted to death by a pack of hounds and a lot of young men on horseback, apparently without any notice being taken of the event by the Society alluded to. Truly we are a funny people.

DEATH OF A CHILD

An inquest was held into the death of the newborn female child of a Brize Norton woman. She stated that she was living apart from her husband, whose whereabouts she did not know. She had told nobody of her condition and made no preparations for the birth because of her circumstances and lack of friends, but had called in two neighbours when the time came. The baby was dressed and put into bed beside her, but was dead when she awoke next morning. She could not account for marks found on the child's neck, and the doctor stated that he could not say definitely how they were caused. The jury returned a verdict of death from asphyxia, but there was not sufficient evidence to show how the asphyxia had been caused.

LESS BEEF THIS YEAR

We understand there will not be as much beef as usual for the annual distribution, the amount of money received by the Bailiffs being less than last year, and nearly a third less than two years ago.

WANTED - HOUSEKEEPER

or wife; no family. John Jewell, Minster Lovell, Witney, Oxon.

WHAT NEXT?

One of the automobile papers has called attention to a want in the villages of the county. The complaint is that there is no name put up so that the passing motorist can see what place he is passing through. Most people will probably think that a road map would be sufficient, but if the motorist cannot delay his speed to study maps he might stop and inquire. If his time is too precious for either of these courses he might defray the cost of putting up names, for it is quite certain that nobody else requires the information. What will be the next thing these road monopolists will wish the ratepayers to do for them?

PEACE AT LAST

Christmas this year will be celebrated under more pleasant conditions than have prevailed for some years past. War is practically absent from this world of ours now, and the trade of the country has recovered from the disastrous effect which war always entails upon commerce, and to which rule the South African war was no exception. Peace reigns, commerce is prospering, and we dare hope that agriculture is improving. May every reader of this journal have a right merry and happy Christmas.

1907

The Government's Compensation Act received a warm welcome from working people everywhere. Another popular piece of news was that a fund was being set up to provide for Old Age Pensions of five shillings a week for people over 65.

Keir Hardie's Women's Enfranchisement Bill was defeated. This led to intensified campaigning by the Suffragettes; many of them were imprisoned as a result of violent clashes with the police. In Finland, by contrast, the first women MPs were taking their seats.

The War Office began to reorganise the British Army and its voluntary branches. Witney's Volunteers were a fine body of men, but there was concern that there were only about 60 of them.

Several alarming accidents in Witney were reported. The motor car remained as unpopular as ever with 'Jottings', who even wondered if its dusty and dangerous presence was putting people off renting the town's unoccupied houses.

There was criticism of both secondary and primary education in the area at the beginning of the year, and in the summer some local children earned reprimands for chalking on residents' doors and stealing fruit from their gardens.

SECONDARY EDUCATION

Secondary education has not received the attention in Oxfordshire that it deserves. Though the County Council has voted some money to help certain schools in the county, there has been no attempt to formulate anything like a system of secondary education in our midst. Farmers and tradesmen can only get a school for their children at a very considerable cost. Nor are the class mentioned the only people who would benefit by better secondary schools than we have at present, for they should be made available to clever children of every class who can afford to pay a small fee. Nay ideally secondary schooling should reach further still and include the clever child whose parents are too poor to pay anything by giving scholarships. The neighbouring counties of Gloucestershire and Berkshire do this by raising a 'penny rate' to pay for it. Why cannot Oxfordshire do the same?

The governors of the Grammar and Technical School have been trying to raise £3000 needed to enlarge the school. The County Council has agreed to provide £2000 if the neighbourhood finds the rest. The Governors have tried everything to raise this money without success. A last effort is now being made by asking the County Council to rate the town and neighbourhood for the £1000, such rating to extend over some 20 years. The amount, it is stated, would not entail a rate of more than a halfpenny in the pound on the town and a farthing on the parishes around which the school might serve. It is very satisfactory that at a public meeting held in Witney a resolution in favour of the County Council rating the town for secondary education was carried by a large majority.

COMPENSATION FOR LOSS OF LICENCE

The following compensation has been agreed to public houses that have lost their licence in an attempt to reduce the number of public houses in any street and to reduce the amount of drunkenness.
Malt Shovel, Witney £761.
Jolly Tucker, Witney £1250.
Fox and Hounds, Nettlebed £550.
Kings Arms, Banbury £1600.
The charges levied on existing licensees in 1906 amounted to £3521 and the balance after paying compensation is £2011 10s 9d..

CURLEW SHOT

Mr Hedley Clack of Gaunt House, Standlake had the good fortune to shoot a fine male Curlew on Thursday. This is a bird remarkable for its long curved bill, and is very uncommon in this country.

ANNOYANCE AT THE POST OFFICE

Considerable inconvenience and much annoyance has been caused at Witney by a new rule of the Post Office, which requires a fee of 4d to be paid by anyone enquiring for letters unless they have a private bag. It appears that since the 5.30 delivery has been abandoned on Tuesdays a considerable number of persons apply to the office for letters, which on other days would be delivered at this time.

It seems that unless a letter is posted before 9am it is now impossible to get it on the same day, indeed not till nearly 9 on the following morning. Surely in the twentieth century the residents of a town in direct communication with London are entitled to get their letters in something under 23 hours after posting without paying an exorbitant fee.

There is one safe way of avoiding mistakes in distinguishing between mushrooms and toadstools.
Eat parsnips.

BOYS BRIGADE
Vs
NIGHT SCHOOL

These teams met on the Brigade ground on Saturday and after a good game the school was defeated by a good margin of six goals to one. The scoring was opened by Hicks for the visitors and soon Kent with a good shot equalised. In a short time he placed the ball between the posts again and just before halftime notched up a third goal. In the second half Lloyd was the only player who could put in a straight shot and obtained three more goals for the homesters, giving them the honours of victory by 6-1.

THE AURORA BOREALIS

A fine display of the Aurora Borealis was witnessed in Bampton throughout Saturday night, from about 7pm to after 10pm. At first the display took the form of streamers which varied in shades, sometimes the colour was brilliant yellow then green and fiery red. The sky was frequently covered with brilliant coruscations shooting up from the horizon and converging in sheets of feathery flame high in the sky. Many of the inhabitants were much alarmed, imagining it was a fire somewhere, and others thought it was a sign that something dreadful was going to happen.

PRESENTATION TO POSTMAN

Upon the occasion of the retirement of Mr. E. Ball from the Post Office service, he was presented by the Postmistress and staff with an easy chair and silver watch guard, with expressions of good will that he would long be spared to enjoy his earned pension. Mr. E. Ball first entered the service in 1869 as a rural postman for Standlake, but when Standlake was converted into "cycle post", in March 1903 he was transferred to East End, Northleigh. During the whole period of 38 years and seven months he discharged his duties with diligence and fidelity.

A BIG PIKE

Mr H. W. Sprenger, while spinning for pike in the Windrush, caught a good specimen weighing 14 lbs 15oz (weighed an hour after being caught), length 36 inches, girth 18 inches.

PUBLIC CONVENIENCE

Mr Dring of the U.D.C. proposed that a committee be appointed to consider the possibility of providing a public lavatory and urinal. He thought it one of the greatest needs of the town. Mr Knight agreed with the proposal, but did not believe in going to any great expense. Mr Smith said the ratepayer had quite heavy enough a burden to bear, but if it could be done as Mr Knight suggested at small cost then they might agree on the matter. They could easily spend a lot of money on a thing of this sort.

POLICE COURT

Hamnal Beban, a tramp, was charged with destroying a rug the property of the Union Workhouse, value 5 shillings. She was further charged with fraudulently obtaining relief while having money in her possession and not disclosing the fact. She was sentenced to seven days imprisonment for the first offence and three days for the second to run consecutively.

THE CROFTS ROAD

To chairman U.D.C.
Dear Sir,
Knowing you will shortly be making a new road in the Crofts we think it would greatly improve the south end if our building fence were set back to the building line of the existing 4 houses. You will see by the plan that so doing it will throw about 103 super yards in the roadway making it about 7 feet wider.
We make this offer now, as it would materially alter the layout of the road and the additional width to the road would be made the best use of.
Yours faithfully,
A.J. & F.C. Williams

WASTED EDUCATION

The Rev. J.O. Bevan complained of children being unfit for agricultural work after leaving school, and doubtless he is right. A very large proportion of teaching in elementary schools is undoubtedly wasted.

Too many subjects are taught and many more than the minds of the children can comprehend, and the result in many cases is they are unfitted for the work they have to do. We know that in saying this we are incurring the displeasure of those who wish to educate every child to the highest pitch possible, nevertheless it is true that every child cannot be educated, nor indeed can the vast majority.

COUNTY COUNCIL ELECTIONS

The following have been returned unopposed : -

Witney – Mr. W. Smith J.P.
Bampton – Mr. F. D. Hunt J.P.
Hailey – Mr. J. W. Abraham.
Standlake – Mark Florey.

In the Rural District Council election there will be no contest in any parish in the Witney Union.

SCRUTATOR

Would like to know

Who is responsible for laying the drain from The Crofts to Emm's Ditch?

And why it is necessary to go 5 or 6 feet deep through solid rock in order to put a surface drain down hill?

If the children who amuse themselves by writing on people's doors and houses obtain their chalk from the school they attend?

If so whether the teachers cannot prevent this purloining of school material?

DUST EVERYWHERE

The advent of fine spring weather is indeed acceptable to everyone after a somewhat long winter, but unfortunately it has introduced the great dust fiend. Last Sunday one of the favourite walks of Witney people, the Burford Road, was rendered quite unusable owing to the cloud of dust raised by the numerous motor cars passing. Indeed this was the case everywhere along the route from Oxford to Cheltenham. Is no step to be taken to vindicate the right of every citizen to the free use of the highway? Month after month, year after year, those demons of the road continue to rush along the highway, raising dust to such an extent as to practically prohibit all other traffic using the roads.

It is quite certain that one of two things must be done, otherwise people will begin to take the law into their own hands. The authorities must either insist that motors must be constructed in such a manner and driven at such a speed as to raise no more dust than ordinary traffic, or they must make roads in such a manner that no dust can be produced. Local Authorities can make their roads dustless. The best plan is for them to adopt one of the methods in vogue on the continent and thus obviate the terrible nuisance that now exists.

We would like to thank the Witney Surveyor for having the Witney streets swept to keep down the dust.

PUBLIC CONVENIENCE

The committee to consider the question of a public lavatory recommended a site under the Town Hall, which would cost £97.

SLOW MAIL
The long way round for the post

The conveyance of the mail from Witney to Swindon has been let by tender for £1 a day. A small sum when everything is taken into account, 2 men, 6 horses and stabling at Witney, Faringdon and Swindon.

Why is this cost incurred? Why should it be necessary to convey letters from London for Witney to Swindon and then send them back 24 miles by road? Why should west of England mails come to Witney by road when we have a railway that covers the whole district? In fact the present system is very like it was when it was inaugurated long before we had a railway, and the Postal Authorities have no notion of reforming their antiquated mode of carrying the mail.

ALMSHOUSE CRISIS

A very serious matter has arisen with regard to the poor Almshouse widows. Holloway's trustees, in selling the property with which the Almshouses are endowed, did not raise enough money to continue the present rate of payment to the occupants, indeed it is said that the weekly payment of 5/- would probably be cut to 2/6. It is quite impossible for these people to live on any such sum and the question arises what is to be done.

There are six almshouses and when they were built nobody ever dreamed that the agricultural depression would reach such a point as to render the income from the charity farm inadequate to provide sufficient to keep the six occupants. Here is a splendid chance for some of those who are blessed with a large share of this world's goods. Some £1400 or £1500 would make up the deficiency and thus render the latter years of these poor widows more happy than they will be otherwise. Who will do it?

In these days of so much sentimental religion it would be a treat to see a little practical Christianity exhibited towards these poor souls, who had every reason to believe that when they obtained an Almshouse they were safe from poverty for the remainder of their days.

THE BUDGET

Mr Asquith's budget appears to be about as expected. Small incomes are to have some relief, while death duty on estates of over £150,000 is to be increased. What is more important to the bulk of the people is that the sum of a million and a half is to be set aside for an old-age pension fund.

The fact that the budget does not greatly please either the millionaire or the socialist would seem to suggest that the Chancellor of the Exchequer has hit it about right.

A GOOD DAY'S RACING

The Berkshire Hunt Point-to-Point steeplechase took place at Barley Park Farm on Saturday. It was attended by a large number of people. Unfortunately the weather was not propitious and for half-an-hour in the middle of the races there was a drenching downpour of rain and hail. Happily the weather cleared up and the remainder of the racing was witnessed in pleasant conditions.

ACCIDENT AT STAPLE CORNER

A horse and cart with a horse tied behind was proceeding round the corner when the horse became frightened by the noise made by a motor tricycle coming behind. The horse pranced and the people passing at the time got frightened, and in the excitement a little girl named Bridgewater fell and the wheel of the cart passed over her shoulder. Dr. Harvey was quickly in attendance, and found no bones were broken, and apparently no serious damage was sustained.

THE HEALTH OF THE TOWN

The medical officer's report must be considered most satisfactory. Great complaint is frequently made of overcrowding in towns. Witncy with a fraction over 4 in a house cannot be said to suffer from that evil. Indeed we imagine that few towns can be found where the inhabitance per house is so low.

Whether the low death rate can be attributed to that cause or not we do not know, but the rate is certainly low, two per 10000 less than the rate for England and Wales. No deaths were attributable to infectious diseases and if tuberculosis [consumption] could be kept away the death rate would be very much lower still.

With such a clean bill of health Witney should become a favourite resort for those whose means allow them to choose their place of residence. The town is now supplied with water as pure as it is possible to obtain. Main drainage has been carried out, and we think we are correct in saying that the cost of living in Witney compares very favourably with that in most towns. How is it that there are at the present time so many houses to let in the place? Something like 20 fairly good sized houses vacant in a small town is not a hopeful sign for either those who have property or for those who trade in the town.

Could it be the motorcar nuisance that prevents people coming to live in Witney? The best roads for either driving [horse drawn vehicles], riding or walking exercise in the neighbourhood are given over to the motorist, and when the weather is fine and the roads dry, no one can either ride, drive or walk on them with any degree of comfort in consequence of the dust to say nothing of the danger to life or limb.

How long will the vast majority of the people consent to allow a very small minority to monopolise the highways?

DARKEST WITNEY

DEAR MR EDITOR, - I nose you allus takes up the cos of the down trod, so I takes the liburty of tellin' you how I was put about the other nite. I was cal'd to go and see Mrs Harris, and wen I got out of my door the Church was just strikin' 12, and the streets wer as dark as a black bull's tale. So I ses Sairey you must walk in the middle of the road, and arter feelin' about with my umbreller I managed to get there, but it was so dark that I couldn't see nothing, but thank the 'evens a flash of litenen come now and then, w'ich just let me see ware I was. Wen I got somver ni the Butter Cross I walked rite into a man's arms. "Wot's yer little game now old gal," says he, and I says "Wot's your game, you rude man." He says "I'm lookin' arter the town." Then I says "W'y don't you lite them lamps," and he says "That ain't my dooty." I says "Dooty be blowd, ow can you see a pore widder a-wanderin' along in Jipshun darkness, and not help her." He says "The 'Counsel' manages the lamps." "Oh! I says, do they, then I should like to 'ave some of them 'Counsels' 'ere, and I'd give 'em a bit of my mind."

Well, I wander'd on, but 'ow I should find Mrs Harris' house I didn't no, for I could see nothin', but as lu'k wud 'ave it, just as I got in front a flash of litenen' show'd me the 'ouse, and then I felt the way as best I cud, but stumbuld over the curb, and smashed my umbreller. Then I felt wot I thought was the dore but it was the winder, and 'twas a mercy I didn't push my 'and through the glass. Then I felt along till I got to the dore, but couldn't find the 'andle, and I was just going to kick the dore wen another flash of litenen showed me the 'andle. So I goes in, and there was that deer criter sitin' up waitin'. Why Mrs Gamp, says she, 'ow frightened you do look. Yes, Mrs Harris, says I, and so would you be if you'd 'ad my journey, it is somethen awful. And then she takes the bottle off the shelf and says, Mrs Gamp, 'elp yourself. So I ses, well, I'll jist put my lips to it. Then I opened my 'eart on them "Counsels", and I ses Mrs Harris wot do I pay rates for? 4/9 in the £ they say it is, and I shall pay 19/- this year, wot for ses I. Wot do I get for my 19/-. I'm not a Rooshan nor a Prooshan Mrs Harris, ses I, but a poor widder, who 'evs to get my livin' by goin' out at all 'ours, fur time and tide, life and death waits fur nobody, not even fur "Counsels" nor moon, nor lamplighters. Then Mrs Harris said Mrs Gamp, 'ave you herd of the sufferers who 'olds meetin's in London, and goes down to Parlement, and pitches inter the pleece. Let's get a sufferers meetin' in Witney, and just let these "Counsels" no our minds.

Hoping you will print this,

Yours obedient,
SAIREY GAMP

TO BE SOLD OR LET-
No 17 Corn Street formerly known as the Malt Shovel. Apply "M" Gazette office.

COGGES

Vagaries of a lunatic

Not a little excitement has existed at Cogges during the past few weeks, in consequence of a man who styled himself a millionaire, taking up his abode in the house of a workingman, who hospitably entertained the stranger. The millionaire wanted horses, carriages and bicycles and orders galore were given; horses tried and bought (not paid for) coachmen, grooms and pageboys engaged. The extraordinary conduct of the stranger was the engrossing topic of the day. Unfortunately the large castle in the air quickly tumbled to earth, for on Thursday the visitor exhibited signs of insanity. Dr. Harvey was called in and certified the gentleman. On the following day the unfortunate man was removed to Littlemore Asylum.

It appears that the name of the man was Harry Wilks, and that he was discharged from the Warwick Asylum in December 1905, and that his place of settlement is Shipton-on-Stour.

NO LIGHTS

Charles Rowles labourer of Hailey was summoned for riding a bicycle without lights. The defendant pleaded guilty.

P.C. Hunt stated that on May 18th he saw the defendant riding a bicycle near the Butter Cross at 11.20 pm. Witness stopped him and asked where his light was and defendant said he didn't know it was out.

Defendant said he lighted it just before he got to the policeman and it must have gone out.

Fined 5/-.

****

COMPENSATION ACT

The near approach of the first of July induces us to remind our readers that on that day practically every man and woman who works for wages will in the event of meeting an accident while engaged in the employer's work, be entitled to compensation from the employer. Hitherto those entitled to compensation have been the men engaged in certain occupations, but the Act of Parliament of last year made it universal.

The inclusion of domestic servants is the most novel part of the new law. Hitherto they have been ignored. There has been no legal liability on the part of the employer to compensate domestic servants, though many thought that there was a moral obligation.

The Act, which compels everybody to do what a few did in a voluntary manner will be welcomed by every one.

A BAD CASE OF NEGLECT

George and Sarah Davis, tramps, were charged with wilfully exposing their children in a manner likely to cause injury to their health. P.C. Dorrell said he found the prisoners sleeping by the river. They were lying on a few rags, and were covered with a portion of their clothing. The children were lying beside them with no covering but a few rags. It was a very cold night. The children were in a filthy condition, and were suffering from exposure.

Mr T. J. Finnis, master of the workhouse, said Agnes May aged 5 was covered with vermin, scantily clad and her feet were in a very bad condition. Herbert aged 4 was alive with vermin, and had a bad sore on his left foot, and one on the right. Charles aged 12 was in a very dirty condition, scantily clad, and had two sores on his right foot which was swollen. Joseph aged 7 was in a verminous condition; he had a bad scar on his right eye, a raw sore on the left heel, and his knee was scorched. The Chairman, in sentencing the prisoners to six months imprisonment, said "It would be a kindness to hand the children over to the Matron of the Workhouse."

SEWER SCARE

It was feared that the sewer in Corn Street might have been broken. On Monday as a locomotive drawing two trucks of stone was passing down Corn Street the wheel broke through the road to the depth of 15 inches. On examination by the council's surveyor the sewer was found to be intact, and nothing worse than a broken water pipe. resulted from the rather extra-ordinary incident.

ROYAL VISIT

The King while staying at Nuneham Park, motored over to Stanton Harcourt on Sunday afternoon. His Majesty spent about half-an-hour looking over the Church, Pope's tower and the Old Kitchen, entering and leaving by the front door of the lodge, the residence of Mr. F.A. Anson, from the grounds of which there is a private entrance to the church. The King was accompanied by several of the house party at Nuneham, among whom were Mr. And Mrs. L. V. Harcourt, and Robert Harcourt. The whole party occupied six cars.

About 100 loyal subjects living in the vicinity were gratified by a sight of His Majesty and were pleased he looked so well. We are glad to say the King was in no way thronged or incommoded: but a hearty cheer was raised as he drove off, which as usual was most graciously acknowledged.

REGISTRAR'S RETURNS

For Witney and nine rural parishes with a population of 72291, the births during the past quarter numbered 39 (21 male, 18 female), deaths 27 (19 male, 8 female). There was one death from violence, one scarlet fever and five deaths occurred in the workhouse. Of the persons who died 5 were under one year and eleven over sixty.

WITNEY TRIP

The announcement of the trip to BLACKPOOL reminds us of the late Mr. E. Smitheman who started the Trips in 1879. The first trip was to Brighton.

The intention of this gentleman was to give the people of Witney an opportunity to visit various watering places and other towns of interest in the country which they had been previously unable to do. Every year a fresh place was chosen, Brighton, Portsmouth, Weymouth, Hastings, Bourne-mouth &c., and when the south coast had been exhausted, Mr. Smitheman fairly took the breath out of the Committee by proposing Bala in North Wales. The committee had discussed the *pros* and *cons* for some two hours and had arrived at a conclusion, when in came a member of the committee who had just arrived by train. Addressing the chairman, he said "I don't know what you have done , but I am dead against Bala." Whereupon Mr. Smitheman rose, and using an unparliamentary expression contained in three words gathered up his papers and made his exit. Notwithstanding this little *contretemps*, to Bala the trip went. Since those days the Trip Committee have for some reason or other fought shy of new places, hence Portsmouth or Southampton have been selected almost every year. This we think is a mistake: the people wish to see as much as possible of the country of which they are proud citizens, hence we predict the Blackpool trip will be popular. The distance, it is true, is considerable but each party of eight persons can have a compartment to themselves, they can surely amuse themselves for a few hours in a comfortable railway carriage. The train will be passing through parts of the country that the vast majority of the trippers have never seen. The route taken will be *via* Birmingham, Wolverhampton, Crewe, and Preston, passing the Manchester and Liverpool canal. The return journey through the Black Country, with its blazing furnaces, will be a weird spectacle altogether new to most of the people of the district.

Death of Mr. L. Shuffrey

We regret to record the death of Mr. L. Shuffrey, eldest son of Mr. L .A. Shuffrey of London, which took place in his residence 63 Woodgreen at the early age of 33. The deceased gentleman came to Witney nine years ago to take charge of the branch works of the firm of Messrs. L. Shuffrey & Co., overmantel manufacturers. For many years the deceased had suffered from heart trouble, which recently had become very acute, and for the last two months he has been lying seriously ill. Notwithstanding the assiduous attention of Dr. Kelly and the visit of a heart specialist he died on Saturday last.

WORKHOUSE OUTING

At the invitation of Mr. and Mrs. Abraham the whole of the inmates of the workhouse who were able to travel went to Ringwood in vehicles kindly lent by Messrs Tarrant & son, Habgood, Midwinter, Mawle, Phillips, Payne and Cooper. Messrs Abraham, Mawle and J. Wisdon lent horses. On arrival the party at once began to roam the beautiful grounds and in a short time tea was served. A capital meat tea was provided and many willing helpers waited on the guests. Tea over, the children were amused with swing cricket, while the older people were seated round the lawn where they were liberally supplied with beer and tobacco, and sweets and biscuits were supplied to the children. Songs were sung by several of the men and by some of the children. A vote of thanks was given by Mr. Daniels, one of the inmates, and the children sang "he's a jolly good fellow" all the way home.

CHURCH PARADE

The Volunteers came out well when they had their Church Parade. It is decidedly creditable to the young men who give their time and a considerable amount of energy in order to be able to take their part in defending the country if unfortunately it should ever require being defended. But a question forces itself upon one when witnessing the procession wending its way to church, and that is Why is there not a larger number of Volunteers?
Some sixty men drawn from Witney and the surrounding district is not anything like the number there should be from such a locality. There are a lot of young men in our midst who would be much more usefully employed spending their spare hours in learning to shoot straight, and the arts of war, than in loitering about doing nothing.

A DANGEROUS MOTOR CAR

Many of the inhabitants of Bampton are complaining of the way a certain gentleman, living a few miles from the town, races his large motor car through it, only a few days ago he narrowly missed running over two little girls in the Market Place.

GRAMMAR AND TECHNICAL SCHOOL

The following have gained certificates in the recent Oxford Local Examination:- Senior third class honours:- V.Rowles, M.M.Clarkson. First division:- H. Blackley, L.Hinton, H.M.Clarkson, E.M.Savile, M.Wiggins. Junior First division:- H.Miller, E.Saunders, T.Painter.

COST OF ROAD REPAIRS

The County Council estimates that the extra cost of maintaining the roads owing to motor traffic is £10,000. The Council has passed a resolution to the effect that the time has arrived when further substantial tax should be put on this kind of traffic. It is only fair that those who wear out the roads should pay for them.

MILITARY MOVEMENTS

The largest number of military troops seen in Witney for many years passed through the town *en route* from Banbury and Woodstock for Standlake. The troops consisted of a detachment of the 1st and 2nd Life Guards, Royal Engineers (telegraph and telephone sections) Army Service corps and Hospital corps. The men looked uncommonly fit and their horses were in the pink of condition. There were several guns and ammunition carriages of the latest pattern. As they marched in open formation it took a long time for the two or three thousand men to pass through the town.

GARDEN PARTY

At the invitation of Mr. And Mrs. J. V. Early about 400 past and present employees of the firm of Messrs C. Early & Co. attended a garden party at Springfield on Saturday afternoon to meet Mr. and Mrs. J. H. Early. The first item was a cricket match between married and single, for once in a way the former had the best of things, the score being married 97 single 27. A capital Punch and Judy show amused the crowd for a long time. Tea was provided in a huge marquee. Walking round the grounds and playing various games pleasantly passed the time. At dusk the grounds were beautifully illuminated with a number of fairy lights. The town band played a good selection of music. The entertainment ended with a magnificent display of fireworks. As they left each guest received a packet of chocolate.

THE COURT
BAD LANGUAGE

Henry Souch, Labourer of Witney was fined 8/- for using bad language.

Harry Woodcock of Razor Hill and Charles Probetts of Newland were each fined 12/-. William G. Eaton, surveyor to the Urban District Council, stated that at about a quarter to eleven in the evening he and his wife were sitting in their front room with the window open, when he heard a torrent of the worst language he had ever heard.

****

Albert Simpson, Veterinary Surgeon of Witney, was summoned by the Inland Revenue Authority for keeping a carriage without having a licence for the same. The bench fined him £5 and 10/- costs. This was his second offence.

VANDALISM

Chalking on the houses of residents in Witney continues unabated. Can nothing be done to stop it? Mischievous children are the authors, and it really is time that an example was made of the urchins who seem to delight in annoying other people. Complaints again reach us of garden robberies. Fruit forms the principal item of the thieves' booty. It is exceedingly annoying to those who have watched the development of their fruit from bud to maturity, to lose it just as they think they are going to gather it in. Let those who detect a garden thief do their duty and prosecute him.

HELP THE WIDOWS

The Witney Rector has suggested at a public meeting held in the Corn Exchange that some of the charity money usually spent on beef for the poor at Christmas might be applied to supplement the small amount now paid to the widows in the alms houses. Formerly they received 6/- a week. Now due to the agricultural depression and the fall in land rents *(see April 1907)* this has been reduced to 3/-weekly. That the poor souls cannot exist on that amount goes without saying. On the other hand the amount spent annually on beef has doubled during the past 30 years. It is quite certain that there are not sufficient numbers of poor in the town to receive beef amounting to considerably over £100. By all means let some of the money go to increase the income the widows receive.

RUNAWAY HORSE

Edwin Pratley of Leafield, labourer was summoned by the police for leaving a horse and cart unattended at West End on the 8th October thereby causing an obstruction.

P.C. Jones stated he saw the defendant's horse with a cart attached galloping along West End. The horse had its bridle off and in running away it knocked down a child in a perambulator and bruised the child's head considerably.

Defendant said he left the horse outside the Court Inn and put a nosebag on him. They had not been in the house five minutes before he ran away.

Fined 10/-.

WITNEY PARISH LIBRARY

The library will be open on Saturday October 19th at the Town Hall 2.30 – 4pm. Books ½d per volume.

LESS DUST

Tarmac is now being used in road making in Witney. Presumably the Authorities are doing this with a view to provide dustless roads, and most people seem to be of the opinion that some preparation of this kind will have the desired effect. Though there is a clergyman of the neighbourhood who says he has bicycled over many miles of such roads and any motor car doing more than 5 miles an hour even on tarred roads raises a considerable amount of dust. If this is the case then the design of motorcars must be changed. The public cannot continue to be subjected to this menace.

FOOTBALL TROUBLE

It seems a great pity that the excellent winter game of football should be spoilt by unseemly behaviour of those who assemble to witness the play. We understand that a very interesting game at Witney last Saturday in which the participators played the game in a sportsmanlike manner, was considerably marred by the rowdy conduct of a portion of the spectators. In these enlightened days surely it is not unreasonable to expect more seemly behaviour.

FOX HUNTING

We are glad to be able to report that the prospects for the season are excellent. Cubs are plentiful and strong, and doubtless there will be good sport for those whose leisure enables them to enjoy it.

ANTI-VACCINATORS

From January next Anti-Vaccinators will have less difficulty in getting exemption certificates. Hitherto it has been necessary to attend a magistrates' meeting in order to get the exemption, and in some cases (not locally) they have been subject to rather uncomplimentary magisterial remarks. The new Act provides that a "declaration" may be made before a "Justice of the Peace".

From the Anti-Vaccinators' point of view this will be good news, as they would much rather object privately than publicly, but will it be good for the public generally? It will probably lead to an increase in the number of objectors, and as there is no question that vaccination is a preventative of that dreaded disease smallpox, the danger to the public may possibly be greater under the new regulations.

COURT LEET

A COURT OF His Grace the Duke of Marlborough was held in the Town Hall on Friday. The Steward A.G. Higgs Esq., presided. The usual transfers and other business connected with the court having been transacted, the old fashioned custom of walking round an apple tree at the Mount was duly observed.

In the evening the tenants and other friends dined together at the Fleece Hotel, under the presidence of the Steward.

WITNEY ORCHESTRAL SOCIETY- FUTURE PLANS

The next concert will be on Tuesday February 11th. The orchestra will number nearly 40 performers and the principal works being practiced under their conductor Mr. H. W. Sprenger are Schubert's "Unfinished Symphony" and "Rosamunde Overture", Wagner's "Tannhause March" Michiel's "Czardas Dances" and Grieg's "Melodies for Strings". Mr Robert West will play Mendelssohn's "Piano Concerto in G minor" (with orchestra) and Mr G.A. Freeth is engaged as solo violinist.

CORN STREET HARRIERS

They displayed good form on Saturday at Bampton where they gained victory 2 – 0 over the home team. They pressed hard all through the first half, but owing to the excellent goal keeping of Oates and a little bad luck they could not score. In the second half when they were again the better team, they succeeded in planting two goals to their credit through the efforts of Harris and Cooper.

WITNEY
Grammar and Technical School

NOTICE OF FREE PLACES, 1908

THE Governing Body of the above Secondary School desires to inform the managers of Public Elementary Schools, the Principal Teachers, and Parents of Scholars that they are offering THREE additional SCOLARSHIPS sufficient to cover the whole cost of the fees for three years beginning in January next. Candidates must be between the ages of 12 and 15, and must have been in regular attendance at a Public Elementary School in the town or neighbourhood during the two years previous to the application being made.

The Scholarship will be awarded after an examination to be held at the Grammar School, Witney on Saturday December 14th, at 10am. The subjects of the examination will be Reading, Writing, Dictation and Arithmetic, and age will be taken into consideration in marking the papers.

Applications to be sent in before December 7th, 1907 to Mr. J. C. Sims, Registrar, New science Buildings, Witney, who will also supply any further information.

(Signed) J. C, Sims,
(Registrar)

November 22nd 1907

RATES RISE

In spite of some protest the Urban District Council has agreed to raise an extra rate for Secondary Education in the town. As is well known the County Council has offered £2000 and the school Governors another £500. Thus only £1500 is needed to complete the necessary total of £4000. The rating would be simple: 2d rate for twenty years would meet the difficulty. Mr Knight as a Governor of the school said that it appeared absolutely necessary that the money was raised, if not they were in danger of losing the school altogether. By a recent order of the Board of Education there would be a number of free places in the school. Twenty five per cent of the school would be open to free scholars of the elementary schools of the district provided they passed the necessary examination. Thus all classes would benefit by the school. Mr Knight hoped that before 12 months had passed that they would have good buildings for the Grammar and Technical school.

******

BARNARD GATE

Proposed new Chapel – for some 21 years the Wesleyan Methodists of the little hamlet of Barnard Gate have met for worship in a mission room in Mr. Webb's cottage, but required a larger place. Mr J.F. Mason M.P. was approached and he readily gave a site near the main road, and it was determined to build an iron chapel.

On Tuesday the foundation stones were laid by Mrs Hopkins, Mrs Beckett, and Mrs W. Webb, and Messrs Hopkins, W. Watts, J. Webb and H.J. Gillet (the latter in memory of Mr Stokes).

The Chapel is being built by Messrs Harrison & Co., of London.

TRAP ACCIDENT

An assistant to Messrs Fowler's was delivering meat at Leys Villas, when the horse bolted and galloped along the road at the top of the Leys, on turning sharply into Station Road the trap capsized and the horse then dragged it on the hub of the wheel until stopped by Mr J. Seacole. Beyond a broken shaft no further damage was done.

BL

SCHOOL CHILDREN ENTERTAINERS

For some years now children from St Mary's schools have given delightful entertainment in the town, and this year is to be no exception. On Monday, Tuesday and Wednesday next there is to be an operetta entitled the "Magic Cup" in the Corn Exchange. The teachers and children with the invaluable help of Mrs. Kelly have been working very hard to make the affair a success, and judging by previous years their efforts will be rewarded with a crowded house.

DON'T BE SWINDLED

Our correspondent sent us a letter, which his wife received from a certain London Tea Company. Accompanying the letter is what proposes to be an award certificate. The certificate entitles the lady whose name is attached to receive a "present", 2oz of tea and seven pieces of genuine silver-plated ware, consisting of six spoons and a fish fork, on condition a postal order for 4/6 is sent with the certificate. We recently saw an advertisement for six spoons for 1/6. We should strongly advise anyone who receives this circular letter, to handle the articles before they part with 4/6, or better still have nothing to do with traders of this kind.

OXFORDSHIRE HIGHEST RATES

The Poor Law returns for Berks, Bucks, Oxon Surrey and (part of) Warwick for the year 1905-6 showed an average of 1/0½d. Surrey came out the lowest with a rate of 10½d while Oxfordshire came out highest at 1/2½d.
As regards Oxfordshire the highest was Chipping Norton with 1/7¾d and the lowest Headington 7½d. The average for Witney was 1/1½d It will thus be seen that although the poor rate (so called) has for several years amounted to 3/6 in the £, only 1/1½d was paid for the actual maintenance of the poor including the cost of pauper lunatics.
For the county the number of lunatics in asylum per 1000 is Oxford 4.8, Woodstock 4.1, Witney 3.8, Chipping Norton 3.6, Thame 3.3, Headington 3.0, Banbury 2.8, Bicester 2.7 and Henley 2.3.
It does not appear that lunacy is due to poverty, as Chipping Norton has three times as many paupers as Oxford yet Oxford has 25 per cent more lunatics, indeed the city of learning has a larger proportion of insane than any other of the 49 unions mentioned in the report.

CHAPEL DEDICATED

A dedication service took place on December 17th, the occasion being the opening of the New Wesleyan Mission Chapel. The service was at 4.30 followed by a public tea to which over 100 people sat down.

****
***
*

1908

Mr Asquith became Prime Minister of the Liberal Government, replacing Mr Campbell-Bannerman, who had to resign for health reasons.

The new Children's Bill, or 'Children's Charter', as it was sometimes called, gave hope to poor children, even those of vagrants: it laid down that all children must attend school. It also made it illegal to sell cigarettes to juveniles.

Industrial unrest came to Witney in May: there was a brief strike by the girls operating the power looms at Marriott's Mills. The Gazette dismissed it in a short paragraph.

Suicide and attempted suicide were still criminal offences. A Witney man who tried to poison himself was taken to court, but was treated in a humane and reasonable way, and was not sent to prison.

Freakish weather hit the area in April. On the 25th there was a blizzard which caused chaos in the town and on the roads.

1908 was the year the Olympic Games were held in London. The magnificent new White City, with its specially-built stadium and exhibition, was a great draw for out-of-town visitors. A special train took no fewer than 973 people from Witney and other local stations up to London in September. Some had problems with the return journey.

Two sporting organisations were formed: the Witney and District Football Association and the Physical Culture Club. On the downside, cricket spectators at a local match were reproached for unsporting behaviour.

A Happy New Year

to all our readers, correspondents, advertisers, and also our critics. May the year just commenced see us all more tolerant of each other's opinions, each giving the other credit for good intentions towards the welfare of the nation and its people generally.

GROUNDLESS RUMOUR OF FIRE

Following his usual custom, Mr. Early had a bonfire for the delectation of his grandchildren and other friends and, owing, it is supposed, to peculiar atmospheric conditions prevailing at the time, it was seen for many miles round, and appeared to be a large conflagration. Rumours got about that one of the Witney factories was on fire, and quite lively times were experienced at the telephone call office next morning, caused by the numerous enquiries from anxious friends of our manufacturers.

ICY MARKET PERIL

Thursday, January 16 was cattle market day at Witney, and in accordance with the order of the Board of Agriculture the Market Place was swilled down with water at the close of the Market, while at the same time the thermometer was some 15 degrees below zero, the result being that in a few minutes the Square was a sheet of ice, upon which a large number of the rising generation proceeded to make slides. Unfortunately, as might have been expected, several accidents occurred, one poor woman sustaining concussion of the brain. We venture to suggest that the life and limb of the people are of more importance to the community than the washing down of a market when the extreme cold would probably kill any germ that might be left there, and that the Surveyor would have been well advised to have foregone this mode of cleansing the market under the circumstances. In case that it was absolutely necessary that this swilling should be done, it surely was the duty of somebody to see that slides were not made on it.

****

DEATH OF A WITNEY MAN IN CAPE COLONY

Doubtless many older Witney inhabitants will remember Mr William Rogers, who emigrated to the Cape 45 years ago, as a young man of 18. His death occurred suddenly this month at Kokstad. He started farming soon after his arrival, and also conducted a small school on the farm. He married a local lady and later bought a large estate in the Bontebok Flats. Overcoming many difficulties, he established very successful sheep and fruit farming businesses. He was also active in politics, and represented the S.A. Party on the Legislative Council for the Eastern Circle.

DEATH OF OLD WORKHOUSE INMATE

Charlotte Morgan, who died suddenly at the Witney Workhouse at the age of 72, came into the Workhouse 63 years ago. She had some eye disorder, and was thus prevented from getting her living; she was however a very useful woman in the House, having recently had the charge of the young children. She was much respected by the officers and inmates.

PENSIONS FOR ALL?

This year's King's Speech mentioned, for the first time, Old Age Pensions. A statesman recently said that these would be given to 'the deserving'. Certainly, but who is to discriminate between the deserving and the undeserving? If we are to have old age pensions, and on the whole it is probably a desirable thing, they must be universal, whether contributable or not, and however the money is found. Will our statesmen rise to the occasion? We shall see.

JUVENILE COLLECTORS' TARGET BEATEN

At the Annual Meeting of the Juvenile Missionary Association, the young collectors attended in native costumes, sang a hymn in a foreign language, and made speeches. The total collected in 1907 was £53-9-5d, and the Chairman announced that if the evening's collection amounted to £6, the previous record of £58-6-1 in 1905 would be broken. This was achieved with a collection of £6-10-7d, and a new record was established.

A CHRISTMAS DINNER

Two labourers were summoned for ferreting for rabbits on December 24th on Mr Mason's land at Eynsham. They pleaded guilty, explaining that they were out of work and needed something for a Christmas dinner, but they were fined 15/- and 7/6.

****

DRUNKENNESS DOWN

At the annual Licensing Meeting of the Witney justices, the police reported that the cases of drunkenness in this district had decreased from 30 to 12. It is more than probable that the great majority of these 12 cases were those of tramps passing through the town. However, in any case it is highly satisfactory that drunkenness has decreased by more than half. There is little doubt that as education advances, and provision is made for the rational recreation of the people, that what has been truly described as our national curse, drunkenness, will disappear.

PETROLEUM LICENCE

Mrs Hudson, of the 'Marlborough', applied to the U.D.C. for a petroleum licence, in order to supply petroleum for motorists. The Surveyor said the proposed place for storage met with the requirements of the act, and the licence was granted subject to the quantity stored being not more than 20 gallons.

SAD DEATH OF WESLEYAN MINISTER

It is our painful duty to report the death of the Rev. Arthur Martin, Superintendent Minister of the Witney Circuit, which occurred with appalling suddenness at his residence, High Street, Witney, at the age of 53 years. His energy, courage, cheerfulness and sympathetic nature won him the friendship and respect of all with whom he came into contact.

CHILDREN'S CHARTER

Under the Bill known as the 'Children's Charter', introduced in the House of Commons this month, juvenile smoking will be prevented. It will be illegal for shopkeepers to serve boys under a certain age with cigarettes or cigarette paper, and police officers will be empowered to confiscate cigarettes from juveniles.

The most important provision of the Bill is that all children, vagrants included, must attend school. This should improve the lives of poor little homeless individuals, who will be sent to industrial schools. It may also reduce the number of adults on tramp, for is not the child the tramp's 'stock-in-trade'? It excites the sympathy of the tender-hearted, to the advantage of its worthless parents. Children under school age, unfortunately, will still have to endure the vagrant's life.

WHIP-TOP MENACE

The Recreation Ground would seem to be the perfect place for the annual spring practice of whip-top spinning, but children seem to prefer to endanger themselves and others by doing it in the street.

****

FATHER FINED

John Godfrey of Witney was fined 5s for not sending his child to school. Defendant said the child was 13 years of age and had made the required number of attendances all but 50, and he thought that was quite near enough and he should not send her to school again.

YOUNG WOMEN'S CHRISTIAN ASSOCIATION

At the annual meeting of the Witney branch of the Y.W.C.A. the Secretary, Miss Agnes Whitehead, reported that the year's weekly activities had included social evenings, Bible studies and needlework, as well as musical evenings, evenings of Shakespeare and talks by Mrs J.H. Early on her Indian experiences and by Mrs Escott on her time in Africa. The balance in hand was £3-18-2½d A junior branch had been started; its 55 members paid a yearly subscription of fourpence.

HOCKEY SUCCESS

The Grammar School Hockey XI played an away match against the Bampton Ladies' team, which resulted in a 3-nil victory for the School.

WHAT ARE THE CHURCH BELLS SAYING?
If you want to please the 'Witney Belles', DRESS LIKE A GENTLEMAN AND BUY FROM The 'Wright' Shop, BRIDGE HOUSE, WITNEY.

ROAD PROBLEMS

One would expect that the rubber tyres of motor cars would do less damage to roads than the iron ones on traps. It is just possible, however, that the abominable spikes attached to the tyres of some cars more than balance any saving accruing to the use of rubber-tyred ordinary vehicles. If road surveyors find that roads are now worn as much as ever, it is a clear case of imposing such a tax on motors as will produce a considerable portion of the money for the up-keep of main roads.

WITNEY CENTRAL CRICKET CLUB

At the Annual General Meeting Mr A.E. Horne was voted to the chair, and complimented the Club on winning the Witney and District League Cup. Mr F. Weller, who played 12 innings and scored 240 runs (average 20) won the bat presented by Mr Hemingway, and Mr A. Turner won the ball presented by Mr Dingle for having taken 42 wickets for 219 runs (average just over 5).

A HARD CASE

A young Oxfordshire Light Infantryman was found guilty in the Police Court of making a false answer in an attestation paper put to him by a Justice of the Peace. When asked if he had ever served in the Royal Navy he answered no, but when a policeman searched his belongings his discharge papers from the Navy were found. The prisoner explained that he was homeless, friendless and nearly starving, and had hoped service in the Army would keep him from want. The Magistrates, though sorry for his destitute condition, were legally bound to punish him, and sentenced him to two weeks' hard labour in prison.

NOTICE
MARCH 26th, 1908
WHEREAS it has come to my knowledge that certain persons have used my name for their trade purposes, I hereby give notice that after this date I shall take proceedings against such persons. Signed, **J. GOULD**

Chimney Sweep, Witney.

'DIABOLO', the game that has taken the Continent by storm, can be had at J.E. & B. Knight's, 20 High Street, Witney.

POST OFFICE - On and after April 1st the public counter at the Post Office will be closed at 8pm. The letter box will remain open as at present for the last mail.

ENTERTAINMENT

Mr Churcher presented a most enjoyable entertainment in aid of the Wesley Guild funds. His able and comic recitations, including 'The Phonograph Dog', 'Evins', 'The Railway Hero' and 'Astronomy Made Easy' were enthusiastically received, as was his rendering of a German's impression of his first motor car ride. Mr C. de Nicholas then entertained with some remarkable conjuring tricks, a ventriloquial sketch and some very clever 'Shadowgraphs'.

THE CHARM AND SIMPLICITY

of Amateur Photography is best measured by the thoroughness with which it has entered into the life of today. I have at the address below a full and fresh stock of the best materials, and give to all amateurs ADVICE FREE. My dark room is at your disposal where demonstrations of many processes are given. This season's plates, papers, films, etc., just to hand.

SEE MY WINDOW before buying your Easter Camera.

RANSOM, CHEMIST, WITNEY.

COMMUNICATION PROBLEM

If a Bamptonian wishes to wire to Witney or Burford, or to speak to people in either of those places, his message has to go to London first and then come back again. Bampton is connected with Witney in all its affairs, civil, criminal and commercial, and why the two places cannot be connected by the quickest mode of communication passes the comprehension of man.

SCHOOL CASE AGAIN

John Godfrey, dairyman, was summoned for not sending his child to school. The 13-year-old had not attended school since the defendant was fined 5/- for the same offence last month. He said his daughter was wanted at home to help her mother; he had brought up a family of 13 and had always sent them to school unless they were ill. Fined 7/6d.

ALVESCOT BRASS BAND

The above Band is open to engagements for the coming season. Club, Feasts, Garden Parties, etc. Terms moderate. Apply to W. Taylor, Sec

CLOSING COMPLAINT

To the Editor of the 'Witney Gazette', SIR - Will you allow me just a small space for a great grievance under which a great many of us are just a trifle sore. I refer to the wretched miserable half hour that has been put on us shopkeepers, both masters and men, during this past week. Is there any need for it. It is this half-hour that makes or mars our evening's enjoyment during the summer months. If we can close in winter at seven, why not in summer? Rather reverse the order of closing, have the 30 minutes in winter. The majority of our employers of the town are in favour of still closing at 7, so that we might try and see if we cannot get all in line for this little boon, both for employers and employed. Candidly, is this half-hour business not a miserable farce, and mere bogey? I think it is.

I sincerely hope that our House of Commons who have passed, and are passing, many sensible little bills, and BIG bills too, will find time to consider and pass into law, that extremely worthy little measure, the Daylight Saving Bill, so that we can have some summer evenings for the shopkeepers, aye, and thousands of other folk, who never have any time to get a little fresh air.

Thanking you for this little space,

I am yours faithfully,

WHY KEEP OPEN.

ROAD ACCIDENTS INCREASE

The Highways Protection League reports that in the past three months 42 persons were killed and 145 injured by motor cars, an increase of 25% and 50% over the same period in 1907. More than double the number of motorists have been summoned in the first quarter of this year than last year. No less than eleven of these road demons ran off after an accident.

BARGAINS - Several SECOND-HAND BICYCLES in good order, from 30/- cash. Eaton's Cycle Stores, Witney.

UNIQUE WEATHER?

The 24th of April, four months after Christmas Eve, and a third of the way through the Spring quarter, and here we are with snow clad, frost bound earth, as though we were in the very depths of winter. Surely the memory of the oldest inhabitant cannot recall such weather on the 24th of April.

FINANCE COMMITTEE.

The Committee has received the following letter:

GENTLEMEN - I beg to make application for an increase in my salary as Collector of Rates. For some time past the work in connection with the office has been considerably increasing, about 150 new assessments having been added to the water collection account. I therefore ask your favourable consideration of my application. Yours obediently, A.J. Shorter.

The Committee recommended extra payment of £20 for water rate collection.

DEATHS

MACRAY - April 20th, at Parahyba, Brazil, while on a visit to her brother, Adela Eleanor, eldest daughter of Rev. W. D. Macray, Rector of Ducklington, aged 47 years.

NORRIS - April 27th, at White House, Filkins, the widow of the late Canon Norris, aged 87 years.

APRIL BLIZZARD

During the great blizzard at the end of last month there were snowdrifts several feet deep. Doorways were blocked so that householders had to dig their way in or out. Carriers either did not venture to come, or were unable to take their vans home. The trains were very late owing to snow on the points. On the Saturday afternoon two traction engines carrying ammunition to Wales got snowed up in Newland, and had to remain in the middle of the road till Monday morning.

An old inhabitant of Witney says that there was a similar storm to that experienced here last month 49 years ago, on April 30th 1859. Another story relates that 75 years ago, on the Sunday after Easter, 14th April 1833, the Vicar of Leafield had difficulty in getting to his service in Northleigh Church by farm cart, because the snow was more than a foot deep.

EXTRA TRAIN FOR MARKET

Will everybody please note that, in consequence of an additional train being put on for the Witney Market, the Witney Stock Sale will, in future, commence an hour later - that is, at 1.15. This arrangement, we understand, will enable buyers to attend both the Banbury and Witney markets without the considerable inconvenience which they have had to suffer lately.

BROCCOLI THIEVES

Three boys were put on probation for stealing broccoli from Mr John Burgin's market garden in Eynsham.

FOR SALE - A useful DONKEY. Apply Eli Benfield, Field Assarts, near Witney.

BOYS' BRIGADE FOUNDER IN WITNEY

The Witney Company of the Boys' Brigade had a signal honour conferred upon them when they were inspected by the organisation's founder, W.A. Smith, Esq., captain of the 1st Glasgow Company and Secretary of the Boys' Brigade. Activities on show were a march past, rifle exercises, a gymnastic display, signalling and bridge building. Captain Smith distributed prizes and expressed a wish to see more Boys' Brigade Companies formed in the town.

A STRIKE

Some excitement was caused in Witney on May 6th by a number of young girls walking down the streets singing and booing. It appears that the cause of this unusual scene was a strike among the power-loom weavers at Messrs Marriott's Mills, and that the booing was for those who continued to work. Next day, we understand that some of the girls went on to work, on the masters' terms.

PHYSICAL CULTURE

A Physical Culture Club has been formed in Witney under the chairmanship of Mr. Goatley. Some 40 people have already signed up as members.

LOST, on Tuesday, May 12th, a GOLD SAFETY-PIN BROOCH, set with one topaz. Anyone bringing same to Mrs John Long, 18, West End, will be rewarded.

WITNEY AND DISTRICT FOOTBALL ASSOCIATION

Thirty people attended a meeting at which a motion to form a Witney and District Football Association was carried unanimously.

CRICKET MANNERS

If old prints representing cricket scenes, when our forefathers wore 'top' hats when playing the game, truly depict what used to take place, it is quite evident that the game then played was not considered so serious an affair as some seem to think it at the present day. It was evidently then a game of recreation and amusement, and after all that is what human nature requires at all times. It is indeed a sorry thing for 'war whoops' to be heard at the fall of an opponent's wicket; it is much more English and far better sportsmanship, to cheer a good performance on the opposing side.

FATHER FINED AGAIN

John Godfrey was fined 10s for failing to send his child to school. He has previously been fined 5/- and 7/6d, and has declared his intention of not sending his child to school.

BEES - Wanted twelve Swarms. Particulars to H. Pritchard, Carterton, Oxon.

DROWNING OR SUICIDE?

There have been six mysterious cases of drowning in the area in the last twelve months or so. Though the Jury's verdict has usually been 'found drowned', it seems likely that in some cases suicide was the real cause. Doubtless many of them are the result of a disordered brain, and those who commit the deed are not responsible for the taking away of life. Experts say, however, that there are many who are perfectly sane who will, under adverse circumstances, commit the rash deed. Is it not just possible that people do not look so seriously upon this matter as they should. The fact is that the man who takes his own life is a murderer, for the law calls it 'self-murder'. To put it upon the lowest ground it is a cowardly way of getting out of one's difficulties.

CLERICAL AND LAY CONFERENCE

At the annual Clerical and Lay Conference for the Witney Deanery, Mr. F. D. How proposed 'That the sanctity of marriage forms the true basis of human society'. Dr. Macray seconded, and a discussion having ensued, the motion was unanimously agreed to.

THE GREAT SNOWSTORM
VIEWS OF WITNEY IN THE SNOW (April 26th, 1908) CAN BE OBTAINED OF J.E. & B. KNIGHT 20 HIGH STREET, WITNEY.

WESLEY GUILD OUTING

On Whit-Monday about 100 members of the Guild and their friends drove to Oxford in brakes, then journeyed to Nuneham by water, lunching on the boat. During an enjoyable visit to the park and wood, some members of the party were so fortunate as to get a close view of the Prime Minister (the Right Honourable H. H. Asquith) as he left the house of Mr. L .L. Harcourt, M.P., his host for the weekend, by motor car.

LOST - A LADY'S FUR, on the 24th inst, between Freeland and Witney. Apply, Mr Tite, High Street, Witney.

DANGEROUS CORNER

A correspondent tells us of a very narrow escape of a lady cyclist at Witney. It appears she was coming from West End with the intention of going up Bridge Street, but just as she got to the bottom of Woodgreen Hill, a heavy motor van came down Bridge Street at a great pace; the lady tried to escape by turning up the Newland road, and in doing so narrowly escaped the motor, and fell on the pavement. As we have previously remarked, this is an exceedingly awkward corner, owing to the junction of four roads, from neither of which can be seen what is coming from the other roads. The pace of any vehicle at that point ought not to exceed six miles an hour, and anyone exceeding that should be accountable for driving to the common danger.

SCHOOL CASE

John Godfrey was fined 15/- for failing to send his 13-year-old daughter to school. This is his fourth fine for the same offence; the Chairman of Petty Sessions remarked that it was a very expensive way of going on.

DOUBLE SKULLING SKIFF FOR SALE, £6; can be seen at 7, Woodgreen, Witney.

4th BATTALION TERRITORIAL OXFORDSHIRE LIGHT INFANTRY

'F' Company orders for the week ending 20th June, 1908. Wednesday - Company Drill; fall in at 8, at the 'Fleece' Hotel. Dress - Drill order. Rifles and side arms must be brought on parade. By order E.N. BENNETT, Captain Commanding 'F' Company.

OLD ESTABLISHED MUSIC BUSINESS -- for immediate **DISPOSAL**; good teaching connection. Particulars of Miss Brantom, High Street, Witney.

WANTED – LAD about 14, to see to pony, clean trap, harness, boots, knives, etc. Apply: S. Shuffrey, 7 Woodgreen, Witney.

****
****

TO LET - THE "BUTCHERS ARMS", Corn Street, Witney, doing a good trade; possession the end of July; small valuation. Apply, 2, Market Square, Witney.

WITNEY BRIDGE

A local gentleman has a document from Messrs Wyatt & Son, Builders of Oxford, dated April 24th, 1822, giving an estimate for the demolition of the old bridge over the Windrush and the building of a new one, for £1247-11s-0d. A later estimate, in August, for additional work, brought the total to about £1,300. It may be assumed that the whole of the summer 86 years ago was spent in the building of the Witney bridge.

WITNEY TRIP

Nearly 400 people visited Plymouth for the annual Witney Trip. Thanks to the Witney Station Master, a well equipped corridor train was, for the first time, placed at the disposal of the committee, and the long journey was made under the best possible conditions. The party left at 5.20, arriving at Plymouth at 11.25. All the places of interest were visited, including the famous Hoe, Eddystone Lighthouse, Dockyard, &c. The return journey began at 8.30, and Witney was reached soon after 3 o'clock.

The general impression seems to have been that the railway journey was the best that the trippers have ever had, but that Plymouth, so far as attractions go, is not to be compared with Portsmouth.

****

POISONOUS SEEDS

Three children from Meeting House Lane were taken ill after eating some laburnum seeds on their way through the Churchyard to the Recreation Ground. One boy's life was in serious danger, but Dr. Harvey's efforts succeeded in restoring him to health. Mr and Mrs Hudson, of the Marlborough Hotel, rendered every assistance to the distressed parents.

There are many poisonous plants, berries &c, but it is highly probable that children are never warned against them. Old dames in their primitive schools used to warn children against these things, but does the present day teacher ever descend to such common things of life?

FOUND - A LAMB, on July 13th. If not claimed within 7 days will be sold to pay expenses. Mr E. Hickman, 76, West End, Witney.

NARROW ESCAPE FROM DROWNING

The children of Mr Finnis, Master of the Workhouse, went to the river near New Mills, to bathe, accompanied by Mrs Whitton, the pro tem Nurse, and Miss West the cook. Miss Finnis, who can swim, somehow lost her presence of mind; some say she was drawn into a whirlpool. Mrs Whitton, a good swimmer, at once plunged in to rescue the drowning child, but the latter clutched her by the neck and drew her under. Miss West, who cannot swim, tried wading in to reach them, but failed. Fortunately Mr Sam Middleton was passing and at once jumped in and pulled out Miss Finnis, and

afterwards, with the assistance of others from New Mills, rescued Mrs Whitton who was exhausted. The usual means of restoration were used and Dr Kelly summoned, and the Nurse gradually recovered. Neither is now any the worse for her misadventure.

ALLEGED ATTEMPTED SUICIDE

A large crowd collected in Corn Street on hearing a report that a man had swallowed rat poison obtained from a chemist's shop. Dr Kelly arrived within half an hour, found that mustard and water had already been administered, and applied the usual remedies. He used a stomach pump with some difficulty; it was, however, successful. The man was charged with attempting to commit suicide and remanded in custody until Petty Sessions on August 6th.

FIRE AT WITNEY MILLS

On July 30th at about 8.30am a fire broke out in the upper floor of the Woodford Mill, where workers were carding and spinning. The Mills Brigade, under Mr F. Middleton, at once operated their steam pumps and standpipes, and summoned the Town Brigade. Capt. Herbert Smith and his men arrived quickly and the town water, which happened to be switched off, was got on in about 5 minutes, producing plentiful water. The flames were quenched, but the roof and interior of the building were burnt out and the machinery entirely destroyed. Damage is estimated at £2000.

GRAMMAR AND TECHNICAL SCHOOL PRIZE DAY

S.C. Goodhart Esq., Master of the Grocers' Company (to which Henry Box, the School's founder, belonged), presented the prizes and certificates at this year's Prize Day. The headmaster reported that 71 pupils had attended this term: 40 boys and 31 girls. The new buildings which would be ready next September would add very considerably to the efficiency of the school and the comfort of both staff and pupils. It was hoped that a school library would be opened next term; he ventured to ask for an annual grant from the Governors and appealed for gifts of money and suitable books.

WOMEN'S BIBLE CLASS

Sister Mary Neck's Bible Class had an outing to Blenheim. At the tea, which followed a visit to the palace, Sister Mary Neck, who is leaving the town, was presented with a travelling bag, as was also Miss Martin, the Secretary.

WILLIAM TRINDER, of Filkins, desires to thank the Lady and Gentleman who so kindly took his daughter, in a motor car, to the nearest doctor, after an accident, on Monday last, at Signett Hill, Burford. W.T. would have liked to thank them personally, but he does not know their names or address.

WORKERS?

Tariff reformers will probably not thank the two gentlemen who paraded the Witney streets making speeches to the effect that they were genuine working men thrown out of employment through the free importation of goods, and singing verses of hymns such as 'Lead Kindly Light'. Their appeals for assistance from their fellow-workers were so successful that these hard working men (?) were enabled to pay a visit to several houses of refreshment before they left the town.

TEACHERS' PICNIC

The teachers of the Witney Wesleyan Sunday School were invited by the Superintendents, Messrs J.V. Early and R. Cutler, to a picnic on Bank Holiday. Conveyances started from Witney soon after one o'clock, en route for the valley of the Evenlode, where a very happy time was spent. At the close of the day a hearty vote of thanks was accorded the Superintendents for the generous way in which they had entertained the teachers.

ATTEMPTED SUICIDE

At Petty Sessions a Corn Street man appeared on a charge of attempted suicide. Dr Kelly stated that he had been present when the prisoner had bought a tin of rat poison from Mr Neave's chemist's shop, and later the same evening treated the man with emetics and a stomach pump for phosphorus poisoning. Supt Hawtin said that a few days later he arrested the prisoner, who said he was very sorry and that he had done a very stupid thing. He was committed for trial at the Oxfordshire Quarter Sessions, and bailed in the sum of £20 guaranteed by each of two sureties and £40 by himself.

****

MOTOR MENACE

A market gardener complains that his fruit has been spoilt by dust arising from motor car traffic, and asks what remedy he has for the loss he has sustained. We arc sorry to inform the gentleman that in this country of freedom and justice he has, at the present moment, no remedy at all. His fruit and other crops may be ruined, his house become unfit for human residence, in consequence of having its windows closed night and day, and he and his family may be driven from the roads he has to maintain, and his lungs may get filled with dust and noxious odours, all caused by this modern juggernaut, and he must meekly bow down before the destroying chariot.

The new Road Union is pressing the Government for legislation to control this odious tyranny in the future, as the Motor Car Act of 1903 is quite inadequate to protect the public. The Union needs help in the form of subscriptions and donations.

SOME 'FOOD' FOR REFLECTION

To the Editor of the 'Witney Gazette'. Sir - The American Consul at Cologne says that the report of the Bureau of meat inspection for the German Empire for the first quarter of 1908, shows that 36,987 horses, mules &c., were slaughtered for domestic purposes. What about protection? Working men don't be gulled, this is the food Tariff Reformers would provide you.

Yours truly,
GOOD FOOD.

DANGEROUS PRACTICES

Who is it that removes large stones from the Rectory wall and places them about the Recreation Ground? They are quite dangerous to twilight strollers. Who is it that makes large holes near the footpath there? Surely it is high time that the depradators were caught and punished.

LIGHTS AT LAST

Although the number of people in Witney who can afford to indulge in the luxury of shooting must be small, most of the inhabitants are pleased to greet the 1st of September, for it is on this day the streets emerge from their summer darkness into the full light of the gas lamps. During the last week in August there were some exceptionally dark nights, but as the 1st of September had not arrived, the town was in a state of darkness not to be equalled, probably, in any village of any size in the country.

RECORD TRAIN FROM WITNEY

A record 973 people went on the trip to the 'White City' - 591 from Witney and the rest from other local stations. The train consisted of a semi-first-class saloon, two 3rd class saloons and 13 other large coaches. The organisation and the weather were excellent and much appreciated by the trippers.

WANTED - a MIDDLE-AGED MAN AND WIFE as CARETAKERS at the Church House. Apply to Mr F. Hayter, 21, Church Green, Witney.

WITNEY MAN'S BRAVERY HONOURED

Mr Samuel Middleton has been presented with a Certificate of the Royal Humane Society, signed by the Prince of Wales, for his bravery in plunging into the river to save the lives of Miss Finnis and her friend. Mr. J. V. Early made the presentation in the presence of the Mill workpeople, members of the firm, Mr. T. J. Finnis and Miss Finnis.

CHINA DAY BY DAY

Miss Loader, formerly a parish nurse, gave a fascinating talk about her work among the Chinese, providing for their medical and spiritual needs. She spoke of the kindness and hospitality of the Chinese, the problems of language and dialects in teaching Christianity, and also of the cruel binding of women's feet. Ancestor worship, she said, causes a hatred of female children: a son assures a Chinaman that his ancestorial worship will be continued. Superstitions are strong: roads follow a zigzag course because it is believed that evil spirits can only go straight.

DROWNED IN A WELL

The 64-year-old landlord of the 'Lord Kitchener' public house, Curbridge, was found drowned in a well in his garden. Dr. Kelly stated that he had been attending the deceased for about a month; he suffered from nervous exhaustion and debility but had never expressed any idea of attempting his own life. The inquest Jury returned a verdict of suicide by drowning during temporary insanity.

NEW MINISTER

A social gathering of Methodists from Witney and other places in the circuit was held to welcome the Rev. and Mrs. B. Stanley and family, and also Sister Edna, into circuit.

SERIOUS CHILD NEGLECT

A woman living in Charlbury, formerly of Witney, was sent to Oxford prison for two months' hard labour, after the Chipping Norton police court heard evidence that she neglected and starved her four children, who were emaciated, filthy and covered in fleabites. Her next-door neighbour described her attempts to help the woman, who never did any cleaning or washing. An N.S.P.C.C. inspector described the dirt and stench in the house and said he advised her to go to the Workhouse, which she did, staying until the court case. The children were well looked after there, though their mother failed to do anything for them. She told the Court that her husband, now absent, drank all his earnings and gave her no money; the Chairman said that her sentence would have been much longer if it had not been for her husband's defection and failure to provide for his family.

CRIMINAL CYCLIST

We note that another hapless cyclist was duly fined at Witney for the heinous (?) offence of riding without a light, and fined the same amount as a drunk and incapable woman.

EXCURSIONISTS LEFT BEHIND

Some 50 of those who went to the White City last month managed somehow to get left behind at Paddington Station. They were sent on by a later excursion train on the Worcester line, some of them going to Handborough Station and walking home in the 'small hours'; others walked from Oxford to Eynsham and then, getting tired, chartered a conveyance; while a considerable number stayed in the waiting rooms at Oxford till the morning and then engaged a brake, which arrived at Witney between 10 and 11 o'clock on Sunday morning.

SUFFRAGETTES GO TOO FAR

Recent proceedings of the Suffragettes create anything but pleasant reflections. In defiance of a law prohibiting any procession approaching the Houses of Parliament when in Session, these noisy women not only organised a procession but invited the roughs of London to assist them to 'rush the House of Commons'. 5000 constables had to be employed to prevent this; businesses were closed and traffic suspended, all at the bidding of a few women who would be much more usefully employed in attending to their domestic duties. The 'velvet glove' system should be abandoned: they should be treated and punished as ordinary criminals. To class them as political offenders is simply ridiculous.

FIRE BRIGADE

A new system of calling the members of the Fire Brigade has been tried out. An electric bell at the Fire Station rings up Messrs. Long opposite, and three cyclists are at once dispatched to summon the Brigade. During the test the glass front of the case containing the bell-push was broken by a member of the Urban Council, and the bell rung; a fire was supposed to be in progress at the Blanket Hall, and the cyclists soon brought all the available firemen to the engine house in a short space of time. The trial was stated to be quite satisfactory. After being thus hastily summoned, the members of the Brigade were hospitably entertained by the Captain, Mr. Herbert Smith, at Derwent House. Mr. Knight later reported to the Council that within six minutes two firemen were on the spot, within ten minutes seven were there, and within 20 minutes all available men were present. As an old fireman he thought this very good work; however, some men were without helmets and fire boots, and he thought it unfair that they were not all supplied with these items. Other Council members agreed.

BOUND OVER

At the Oxfordshire Quarter Sessions the Witney labourer accused of attempting to commit suicide on July 26th was discharged on his own recognizances to come up for judgment when called upon during the next 18 months. During that time he would be under the supervision of the Probation Officer. The Court heard that he had been working well, and had letters from the Rector of Witney and the Court Missionary.

PENSIONS QUERY

A correspondent asks if a pensions officer is entitled to ask an applicant for the Old Age Pension whether he has ever been in prison. We know not what the officers' instructions are, but it is highly improbable that they include such an insulting question. We should be greatly surprised to hear that such a question has been asked; if it has, we should recommend the person who has been so grossly insulted to represent his case to the Old Age Pensions Committee.

****

TO LET, No. 37, Woodgreen, Witney, a very pleasantly situated HOUSE; rent £20. Apply to Sam. Shuffrey, 7 Woodgreen.

The **PARISH LIBRARY** will open on Saturday, November 7th, at the Town Hall, 2.30-4pm. Books of all kinds one halfpenny per volume, per week, to suit everyone. Catalogues may be obtained.

'HUNGRY MARCHERS'

A body of men, between 20 and 30 strong, entered Witney, from Oxford, en route, it is said, for Northleach. They had a kind of van with them, from which they addressed an audience on Church Green, on socialistic matters not of the mildest form. They then proceeded to the Workhouse, smoking their pipes, where the Master declined to admit them, unless they were destitute; he offered to admit any destitute person, and allow him to depart next morning, if he could show he was a bona fide traveller in search of work. Presumably they were unable to comply; they went back into the town, and were allowed to sleep in a large room at the 'Plough' Inn.

SPORTING ACCIDENT

Mr. J.F. Mason, M.P., of Eynsham Hall, had a narrow escape from serious injury while on a shooting party at Swan Hill Farm, Hailey. Sir Algernon Peyton stumbled over a furrow and his gun went off. Several gentlemen were injured in various parts of their bodies, but Mr Mason, who was nearest, received no less than ten shots in his face. Despite profuse bleeding, he insisted on finishing the day. We congratulate him on his marvellous escape from what might have been a terrible accident.

FISH DISPUTE

Witney, it seems, rejoices in two fried fish shops, one at each end of the town. The owner of the one in West End objects to the Corn Street proprietor vending his fish from a cart in West End. One remedy would appear to be for him to get a cart and retaliate by hawking his fish in Corn Street. What would be more profitable, however, to both firms, and certainly more pleasant for the inhabitants, would be for each to stay at home and let their customers send for their fish. What a tremendous obstruction would be caused in our streets if all the traders paraded the town with horse and carts.

ACCIDENT TO UNFORTUNATE MAN

Three Cheltenham furniture vans, drawn by a powerful traction engine, were proceeding up Bridge Street, when a horse and cart belonging to Messrs Clinch & Co, of the Eagle Brewery, approached. The horse, owing probably to the fearful noise created by the traction engine and vans, became restive, and in plunging broke both shafts of the cart. Two men were precipitated to the roadway. Unfortunately a barrel fell on one of them, Ernest Clements, and he sustained a broken thigh. He had only been back at work for a few days after being laid up with a broken leg.

DANGER OF PLAYING WITH FIREWORKS

Some small Cogges boys were playing with a toy cannon when a bigger boy proceeded to show them how it worked. The cannon went off, and so severely injured his eyes that he had to be taken to the Oxford Eye Hospital. It is hoped the poor boy's sight may be saved.

GOAT FOR SALE, in kid by Pedigree Anglo-Nubian, 35/-. Mitchell, Carterton, Clanfield, Oxon.

HIGHER TAX PLEASE

It is not often that we fall in with what Tariff Reformers say, but we most heartily agree with Mr Edge, a motor car manufacturer, in his advocacy of a substantial duty on imported cars. The higher the duty the less cars we shall have to annoy the inhabitants of the county and the other users of the roads.

A DANGEROUS PRACTICE

Two Northleach residents were fined 10/- and 5/- for wilfully exposing themselves while suffering from scarlet fever. This case should be a caution to others afflicted in a similar way. There is no excuse in the present day for spreading diseases. The sanitary authority makes every provision for those who are isolated, and it is absolutely necessary that they observe the instructions given them.

BISHOP'S VISIT

The Bishop of Stepney, popular Chairman of the Church of England Men's Society, spoke to Witney members. Never before in the memory of the oldest inhabitant has the Corn Exchange been so packed with men. The Bishop's visit was all the more appreciated because he is Archbishop-designate of York, which entails a greater volume of work and more responsibilities.

PIGEON SHOOTING will be held at 'YE OLDE SWAN', Minster Lovell, commencing at 11am on December 26th. Rabbit shooting and Football Match also.

BUTTER CROSS IMPROVEMENTS

During the last few weeks the Butter Cross has undergone a complete renovation. The roof has been repaired, etc. and the clock tower repainted, etc. The lettering placed on the North side, in bold gilt letters, reads thus: 'Erected by Guiliermus Blake, Armiger, de Coggs, 1683'. We congratulate Dr. Kelly and Mr. Story, the Bailiffs, who have had the work done, on the improved appearance of this ancient building. The date, of course, is that of the erection of the clock tower, the building being, we should imagine, very much more ancient.

POLICE ACT IN FISH DISPUTE

The Council has received the following letter: Sir - Caravans and Fried Fish: I beg to acknowledge the receipt of your letter of the 14th inst on the above subject, and to assure you that I shall, at all times, be pleased to assist your Council's surveyor in carrying out the bye-laws. With reference to the Fried Fish case, I have already given instructions to my men to see that no obstruction is caused, and the owners have been cautioned.

I remain your obedient servant, E.H. Hawtin, Supt.

LOOK OUT!

RABBIT COURSING will take place at the NEW INN, MINSTER, on BOXING DAY, at 11 o'clock.

FOR SALE - Light Single BROUGHAM, little used. On view at 'Findon', Woodgreen, Witney. Price £25, including accessories.

VOLUNTEER DINNER

At the annual dinner of the 'F' Witney Company, 4th Battalion Oxfordshire and Bucks Light Infantry, Dr. Kelly proposed a toast to 'His Majesty's Forces', and expressed a wish that more men should join the Witney Corps. Compulsory service would be a fine thing - for young men to have two or three years' training just as they were growing into manhood, would provide the country with a smart set of men, and, he was sure, improve the English race in a way that it needed improving (applause).

Responding, Captain Bennett pointed out that while the continental papers were full of it, our newspapers now seemed to reflect little interest in compulsory service. People did not seem to realise what an invasion would mean to this country. The Territorial scheme so far had only 200,000 members, full war strength being 316,000. He appealed for more Corps members; once there had been 134, but now there were only about half that number. He was sure Witney could do better.

FARMERS TO COMBINE

At a well-attended meeting at the Town Hall, a resolution was carried to form a local branch of the Berks and adjoining Counties Dairy Association.

BREAD AND BEEF

The Bailiffs have distributed bread and beef in the Corn Exchange to some 700 people.

DRAMATIC PERFORMANCE

The members of the Girls' Circle are to be congratulated on their performances of 'Cinderella' and 'Sleeping Beauty'. There was a good attendance and warm applause for the performers.

1909

Money was a dominant theme both nationally and locally. There was jubilation all over the country when the first Old Age Pensions were paid out in January. However, Mr Asquith's Liberal Government was having great difficulty with its financial policies. The Chancellor, Mr David Lloyd George, wanted to raise taxes in order to pay for rearmament and pensions. His 'People's Budget' was rejected by the House of Lords, many of whose members felt very threatened by the higher rates of income tax and the 'socialistic' thinking behind the proposed measures. A General Election had to be called for January 1910, and hostility between the Commons and the Lords became bitter.

Witney pensioners were happy to collect their weekly five shillings. The Bailiffs, however, were increasingly worried about another matter: the Witney Charities. They felt that they, and the town, had to face up to the fact that the Christmas Bread and Beef was being distributed, not only to the poor, but to a good many people who could well afford to buy their own. Their very diplomatic letter to the Gazette suggesting improvements to the system had a mixed reception.

The New Year has dawned upon us and we hope that it proves a happy one to all our readers. Certainly its advent has been attended with a large amount of happiness to one class of person, the old age pensioner. As these lines are being penned the Post Offices are busy handing over the first week's pay to the deserving old people. Hearty congratulations to all who will this day draw their first five-shilling pension.

One pensioner declared that he had indulged in singing all the next day after receiving his pension.

BREWERS' SUPPER

On Saturday evening the employees at the Eagle Brewery had their annual supper at the Bull Inn, when an excellent repast was served by Mrs. Howell in her usual good style. The chair was taken by Mr. Bliss. Some capital songs were sung and shortly before 11 o'clock three cheers were given for the firm and also for the chairman. The National Anthem and Auld Lang Syne brought one of the most successful evenings to a close.

PRAISE FOR THE POSTMEN

We congratulate the Postmaster and his officials on the punctuality in delivering the letters and parcels at Christmas tide and the New Year. Several of the rural postmen had no easy task to get their letters to the outlying districts, having to walk several miles through snow, being unable to use their bicycles.

WITNEY "BREAD AND BEEF CHARITY"

To the Editor of the "Witney Gazette"

Sir, – It has recently been part of my business as Rector to read the Trust Deed of the "Freeland Charity" a portion of the income of which is paid to the Bailiffs and eventually distributed in Bread and Beef at Christmas. The Deed states explicitly that the money is for the "poor" of Witney. It is however a matter of common knowledge that many besides the "poor" receive the Bread and Beef, and it would be an affectation to pretend that all the six hundred and more recipients could be described with any accuracy as those who are in need.

No doubt many receive the "Bread and Beef" under the impression that as old inhabitants they are entitled to it quite apart from any question of poverty, and this is probably the reason why the list of names has grown the way it has. But I believe there is no ground for any such idea, and that the money dealt with by the Bailiffs is meant *exclusively for the poor, -* certainly this is the case with the portion that they receive from the Freeland Trust.

The result of the present system of distribution is that the really poor are to a large extent deprived of the full benefit of the Charity, and it is on their behalf that I venture to suggest that some new method should be adopted. The aged who are past work, widows, families passing through some time of stress by reason of sickness or unemployment - these and others in like need might receive substantial assistance from the Charity at the time of the year when poverty presses most hardly, if the intention of the Trust were strictly carried out. As in a matter like this a sound public opinion is the one thing needed to secure reform, may I be permitted to suggest to those who have hitherto received the Charity not because they needed it but because they thought they had a right to it, that they should ask the Bailiffs to remove their name from the list? This will not only make the work of the Bailiffs next year much easier, but will also set free funds which will help to lessen the anxieties and cheer the hearts of those among us who know only too well what real poverty means.

Such self-denying ordinance, self-imposed, will be most praise-worthy, and I am confident that many who thankfully recognise that they are not really necessitous, when once they understand the position, will welcome the opportunity of doing their part in restoring to their less fortunate neighbours that larger share of this Charity which rightly seems to belong to them.

In offering these reflections on a difficult subject, I would guard myself against seeming to impute in the least degree any kind of blame on anybody. It is obvious to all who live in Witney that the Bailiffs from year to year have most anxiously endeavoured to administer the Charity to the best purpose. The present need is simply such a healthy public opinion as will enable the Bailiffs in future to feel that they will have the confidence of the town in distributing the Charity on a different principle from that which has prevailed in the past.

Believe me, dear Sir,
Yours very faithfully,

J. B. KIRBY.

DEATH OF AN OLD TRADER

We regret to record the death of Mr. Edward Lower who for more than 30 years carried on a business as a boot and shoe factor on the Hill. The deceased gentleman, who was of a very retiring disposition, was much respected by all he came in contact with.

FALLING BIRTH RATE

A report has been issued by the Registrar General on the serious matter of the lowering of the birth rate.

I do not have the statistics to prove it, but there is no doubt that the decrease in the birth rate is not because children are not born to the poor man but because they are not born in such numbers to the richer and middle classes. Who will deny that this is a calamity? Are not the most of the virtues of our race in the main, with the middle classes? We are therefore by our modern methods, as it seems to me, doing our best to prevent the birth of those who will be capable of performing the highest service to the state. Why so do you ask? I say in reply that the children of the poor are, in some measure clothed by charity, certainly their education is free and in some instances they are fed. There is as a matter of fact very little responsibility attached to the production of children amongst the class I have mentioned.

SUCCESSFUL CONCERT

The Witney Orchestral Society continued its successful career with a concert in the Corn Exchange. Ever since it was founded in 1905 the society has met with the encouragement it deserves.

LOWELL'S PLACE

The Committee reported to the Council that the roadway had been repaired and is greatly improved. We also find that several houses have been thoroughly overhauled and advantage taken of the town water and sewer. Other houses badly require a more efficient water supply, they are drawing from one well and as slop water is continually thrown on the gardens surrounding the well, it is desirable that town water is laid on. We are given to understand that the owner of these properties has given instructions for this work to be done. Generally with the addition of a few further improvements, the whole locality is in a fairly satisfactory condition and no serious nuisance is apparent. Mr Dingle said that the houses at the end of Lowell's place were lower than the sewer and therefore it would be impossible to connect them.

THE KING IN BERLIN

The King's visit to Berlin is a happy augury of a better feeling between the people of both England and Germany. Our sovereign has always been noted for his tact in dealing with every subject that comes his way. If only certain newspapers could be induced to cease magnifying little differences into grave misunderstandings, there would now be a good hope of arriving at a reasonable understanding that would rebound to the best interests of both countries.

WORKHOUSE ON FIRE

A serious fire occurred at the workhouse. A fire was burning as usual in the office fireplace during the morning. At about 2 o'clock in the afternoon the floor of the office was found to be in flames. The Master and the other officers immediately commenced to extinguish the flames with buckets of water, and when these were subdued it was found that the fire had a great hold on the floor and that the beams that carried it were well alight, and in fact the fire had found its way through to the ceiling of the room underneath which was unoccupied. It is thought that a live coal had dropped on to the wooden floor and burned its way through to the beam that supported the floor. Owing to the prompt action of the officers of the house there was no need to call the fire brigade.

DISAGREEMENT ON TREE CUTTING

The tree cutting is being carried out on Church Green in accordance with the advice of the experts consulted. There will of course be differences of opinion as to the mode of pruning, and not a few think the beautiful trees have been ruined. As we suggested some time ago it would be far better to follow one of two courses: either turn the trees into pollards or cut down alternate ones.

WITNEY MAN AS CAPTAIN

On Saturday 13th an international Amateur Football match between England and Germany will be played on the Oxford city ground. Mr Herbert Smith of Witney will captain the English team.

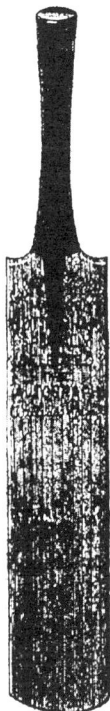

WHAT IS A WITNEY BLANKET?

An action pending concerning the title of "Witney Blanket" is one of great importance to Witney. We cannot comment on it as the case is *sub judice.* The "Drapers Record" has the following: "For a considerable time the blanket manufacturers of Witney have been agitated by the controversy which has arisen in regard to the significance of the term "Witney" as applied to blankets.
It is of course indisputable that the word Witney has been utilised in connection with goods produced in parts of the country far removed from Oxfordshire, and the contention of the manufacturers responsible for this practice is that the term "Witney" has acquired a secondary and "generic" significance and does not necessarily indicate that the blankets to which it is applied are made in Witney.
The group of Witney manufacturers are, however of a different opinion, and, as the outcome of long continued discussion, are about to initiate an important test case in the London Courts. The Prosecutors are Messrs. Chas. Early and Co, Messrs. W. Smith and Co. Limited, and Messrs. Marriott, the three largest concerns. The defendants are Messrs. Ryland and Sons, Limited, Manchester and London. The summons has been issued and will be heard in the Guildhall in April".

ROAD WIDENING

The entrance to Mill Street is an improvement on which the Urban District Council is justified in spending ratepayers' money. This particular spot has been a source of much annoyance and danger to all who use the road. The width of it effectually prevents any decent footpath being made, and the number of pedestrians using the road several times a day certainly calls for some improvement. Besides the convenience to Witney inhabitants, there will probably be an increase of motorists who will go that way to Burford and Cheltenham instead of using the High Street and Corn Street, where inhabitants have hitherto suffered much from motor nuisance.

DUST EVERYWHERE

During the past few days the dust has been intolerable; goods in shops have been spoiled, as well as the dresses of individuals; and householders have had to keep their windows closed, thus keeping out the fine spring air, which has been blowing. Why has the water cart not been used to keep down the dust? What on earth do people pay rates for, if they cannot have their streets kept in a decent state? Possibly the surveyor may have a good reason to give for the state of things prevailing: the ratepayers are certainly entitled to know what it is.

MINIATURE RIFLE CLUB

A well-attended meeting was held in the schoolroom to consider the advisability of forming a miniature rifle club. Every man ought to be able to take part in the defence of his country, and a club of this kind would qualify them to perform part of that duty.

CONGREGATIONAL CHAPEL

The Chapel has undergone a complete renovation. The walls and woodwork have been washed and painted in a light shade of green. New choir seats have been erected on one side and now half face the congregation. A portion of the chapel has been curtained off to form a cloakroom. The vestry and old Meeting-house in Marlborough Lane have also undergone repairs and improvements. The total cost was close on £100 of which £70 has so far been raised.

The Congregationalists are to be congratulated upon making an improvement, which might with advantage be adopted by every Church or Chapel, that is to provide a cloakroom. All have at times experienced the inconvenience of having no proper place to put their hats, cloaks and coats in places of worship. Hats are in danger of getting more or less damaged, and cloaks and coats especially when wet are a nuisance to those who have to sit near them.

***

The tree cutting on Church Green will not please everybody. Some people will bark.

STAINED-GLASS WINDOW

On Easter eve in Ducklington Church a stained-glass window in memory of the late Miss A.E. Macray was unveiled by the Archdeacon of Oxford. The window in the eastern part of the south transept was much admired and is a fine example of the stained –glass art. The inscription is:

To the glory of God and in memory of Adela Eleanor Macray died at Parahyba, Brazil on 25th April 1902.

WHEN IS A BLANKET A WITNEY BLANKET?

After many days of evidence the case brought by the Witney Blanket Manufacturers against Messrs Ryland and Sons under the Merchandise Marks Act has come to an end. The case rests on the problem of whether a blanket made in Yorkshire or elsewhere can be called a Witney Blanket. The judgement has been made that it must be made in or near Witney to be a Witney Blanket. Messrs Ryland and Sons were fined 40 shillings and ordered to pay the plaintiff's costs of £100.

THE ARMY IS COMING

There seems a probability that Witney and district will be well within the area of the autumn manœuvres. We understand that inquires have been made as to the water supply of the district with a view to establishing a camp near the town. It is hoped that every facility will be accorded the military authorities in the matter. Apart from the benefits accruing, from the business point of view, we are sure the general public in this district will welcome "Tommy Atkins" as heartily as would the inhabitants of any other portion of Great Britain.

A THIEF

Henry William Smith of Witney, printer was summoned by the Witney Gas Company for feloniously stealing gas by disconnecting the inlet and outlet pipes of the meter and coupling them together so that gas did not pass through the meter. The magistrates retired and on return to court the Chairman said they considered the case a very serious one. But they dismissed it as the Gas Company could not produce any evidence as to how much gas was stolen.

DANGEROUS MOTORISTS

We observe that a Witney constable has succeeded in a conviction against a motorist for not carrying a light in the middle of the night. When can we expect a prosecution for driving a car above the speed limit or to the danger of the general public?

VAGRANTS

Two tramps were brought up in custody, charged with exposing their six children in such a way as to cause unnecessary injury to their health, at Curbridge on April 19th. They were further charged with wandering from place to place with their six children and preventing them receiving efficient elementary education.

P.S. Longshaw stated that on 20th April, at 12-30 a.m., in company with P.C.Fisher, he found the two defendants, with their six children sleeping in a barn at Caswell farm, Curbridge. The children's clothing was wet, and the witness considered they were exposed in such a way as to cause them unnecessary injury to their health.

T. J. Finnis, master of the Workhouse stated that he saw the six children. Their bodily condition was very good indeed. Their clothing was bad, and they were full of vermin.

Supt. Hawtin stated that he had known the prisoners for ten years as habitual tramps. Since 1901 they had continually travelled about the county with their children. During the past three months he had had complaints from farmers as to tramps.

The male defendant said he had tried many times to get a house but had failed. He formerly lived at Sutton Courteney, and was turned out of his cottage, and had not been able to get one since.

Sentenced to six months imprisonment.

Jottings Comments

The case of the parents is well nigh helpless. It seems that the legislature can do nothing to raise these people from vagrancy. But the law now holds out a hand to the children of these nomads, and lifts them out of the awful life which but for this merciful piece of legislation would surely be theirs. This law means imprisonment for the parents and the removal of the children to clean and healthy surroundings. This is the only way to root out the evil of vagrancy, which has increased so enormously. If the state can only get hold of the children and bring them up to live decent lives the profession will soon die out, and the general public will be relieved from the danger that is a continual menace to farmers and any dwellers in our rural districts.

Hill Rise,
Witney
7th May 1909

To
Mr. H. L. Cole,
120 Corn Street,
Witney.

Dear Sir,
I write to express my deep and sincere regrets for the pain and annoyance caused to you and your friends by your arrest by the police in Witney, on Thursday last, on a charge of stealing my bicycle.

The bicycle was removed by you from outside the county court under a misapprehension that it belonged to your firm (Messrs. Valentine and Barrell) and I am convinced that you had no idea of dealing with it in any unlawful manner.

In a moment of irritation I communicated with the Police, with the result that you were for a short time in custody.

I deeply regret my action and its consequence and tender to you my apologies for conduct which I cannot in calmer moments justify or defend.

I know your character to be beyond reproach and authorise you to make whatever use you wish of this apology and undertake to pay all costs and expenses you have been put to in the matter.

Yours truly,
W. G. PHILLIPS.

———————

120 Corn Street,
Witney.
12th May 1909.

Dear sir,
I am in receipt of your letter of the 7th instant. I accept your apology and regard the matter as ended.

Yours Truly,
HEDLEY LEWIS COLE.

Mr. W. G. Phillips,
Hill Rise,
Witney.

CHILDREN AND TOBACCO

Some dealers in the neighbourhood appear to be putting a different construction upon the Juvenile Smoking Act which the legislation never intended, and which the Act certainly does not justify them in doing. We have heard of more than one case where the dealer has refused to serve children with tobacco for which their fathers had sent them. Dealers should remember that the Act says distinctly "a person shall not be guilty of the offence of selling tobacco to a person under the apparent age of 16 years *if he did not know, or had no reason to believe that it was for the use of that person*". It is quite clear then that when a man sends his child for his tobacco the dealer shall not refuse to serve him.

ROADS

There have been no tenders for certain parts of the highway for the horse drawn haulage of road gravel, and the Council has had to fall back on traction engine haulage. There is a great saving in using these engines, but we imagine that these huge engines with their trailers do as much damage to the roads as the saving effected. Then there must be the greater cost of spreading the gravel on the roads, when it is shot down in huge lumps instead of being deposited in even cartloads all along the length of the road to be repaired.

**

Horses and cattle straying on the highway appears to be on the increase. Time was when the police were very keen to prosecute in these cases, sometimes unnecessarily so, especially when there was plenty of room on common land adjoining the road. Now no one seems to interfere, although the animals may frequently be met with on narrow roads where they obstruct the traffic.

NEW PULPIT

Mr. L. A. Shuffrey of Welbeck St. London has given a new pulpit to Holy Trinity Church, In memory of his Father and Mother. The design is a handsome one and will be a real improvement to Holy Trinity. The pulpit will be made entirely in Witney by Mr Shuffrey's firm.

RECREATION GROUND

The Recreation Ground will be opened for games on the 3rd July. The committee we understand are busily engaged in making final arrangements. Witney people will soon be able to enjoy a game of tennis, croquet or bowls. Everything is being done for the enjoyment of the ratepayer, and it will be their own fault if they do not take advantage of the arrangements that have been carried out by the council. As we understand the charges are to be merely nominal.

TRAINING HOME COMES OF AGE

It is 21 years since the Aston Training Home was opened by Mrs Clarke. At the time the venture was considered a bold one, and there were those who predicted for it a short life. However under the excellent management of Mrs Clarke who has been loyally supported by many friends, the institution has gained its majority, and that lady has the satisfaction of looking back on 21 years of useful work at this home. During that period hundreds of girls have passed through the home and are holding good positions in many parts of the world. We congratulate Mrs Clarke on her work, which has been the means of helping those who have had the advantage of training under her, to secure a higher position on life's ladder than they could have gained without her help.

GOOD DIVIDEND

The Directors of the Metropolitan Bank have decided to pay an interim dividend for the past half year at the rate of 15% per annum free of income tax.

DEATH OF EDWARD MILES

The death of Corporal Edward Miles of Witney, removes from our midst an army veteran who had seen a great deal of active service. He went through the long and dreary campaign in the Crimea, where disease and battle claimed so many victims. He was one of the gallant men who composed the "thin red line" that faced without flinching the perils of the mutiny, and despite treachery beyond belief saved the continent with its teeming millions from being rent in twain by internal strife.

It is to men like Corporal Edward Miles that England owes so much, and gives so little. After fighting 21 years for his country, discharged with a good character, Corporal Miles' pension was so small that he had to work hard to get himself a living. Fortunately he found work, but many of his fellows who fought side by side with him (Empire builders every one), to rich England's shame be it said, had to eke out a miserable existence on parish pay.

On Saturday 3rd July the Urban District Council officially opened the recreation ground.

DUST

Complaints have reached us from Bridge Street with reference to insufficient watering of the street. There is no doubt that Bridge Street gets more traffic than any other part of town, and it is therefore important to the inhabitants that they should receive special attention in the matter of watering. The dust nuisance in Bridge Street on Thursday 22nd we are informed was almost unbearable.

SCHOOLS REOPEN

The Council Schools which have been closed for several weeks owing to an outbreak of Scarlet Fever were reopened on Monday 19th.

MILITARY MANOEUVRES

The military authorities have just issued a map of the coming autumn manoeuvres. The area is an exceedingly wide one, Highworth is exactly in the middle, so Witney should see some mimic warfare.

BOYS BRIGADE CAMP

The 1st Witney Company of the Boys Brigade for the 3rd year in succession spent their annual camp by kind permission of the Military authorities at Golden Hill Fort near Freshwater, Isle of Wight, from Thursday 22nd July to Thursday 29th July. The weather this year was more unfavourable than on previous occasions. The wind was exceedingly rough, but this did not mar the enjoyment to any great extent, and once again the 1st Witney can claim to have had a "ripping time".

OLDEST INHABITANT DIES

The death of Mr Matthew Talboys removes from our midst one of the oldest inhabitants of the town. He was the last surviving member of the original Witney Band, under Bandmaster Thomas Clarke and afterwards Bandmaster A. Titcombe. The deceased was a member of the band that formerly led the singers at St. Mary's Church. Subsequently he became sacristan at St. Mary's and afterwards cemetery keeper. His cheerful disposition and urbane manner won him many friends.

WITNEY UNION WORKHOUSE

At the monthly meeting of the Board of Guardians a letter was read from the Oxford Eye Hospital suggesting payment in the case of a patient in receipt of relief from the Witney Union, who had been an inpatient for three weeks. The clerk was directed to reply reminding the hospital authorities that the Board contributed five guineas a year to that institution.

MOCK WAR

Military officers have been staying in Witney completing arrangements for the coming autumn manoeuvres. It appears that Park Farm will be used as an encampment for 15000 men (mostly mounted) so it is probable that Witney will be in the thick of these military operations.

RURAL DISTRICT COUNCIL

Mr M. Florey complained that the stench from the Witney out-fall works was horrible. He called it a disgrace to any town.
Mr Holtom agreed it was very bad and something ought to be done about it.
The Chairman said that he had inspected the place with Mr Stallard the County Surveyor, but it was found that nothing could be done.
Mr Luckett said that the reason why the nuisance was so bad on some days was probably due to the cleaning out of the septic tanks.

ROAD SIGNS

Now that there is a large amount of motor traffic from Cheltenham and Gloucester, we suggest that a danger sign should be placed at the bottom of Union Hill (Rozer Hill) near the cemetery, in order that motorists should slow down when passing the crossroads leading from Curbridge Road, Dark Lane and Ducklington Lane. When coming down the hill it is impossible for motorists to notice the crossroads, the consequence is seeing a straight road in front of them, they go at such a pace that it is absolutely dangerous to those coming from these roads, and are equally unable to see what traffic is passing at this point until they are right upon it.
It has been found necessary to erect one of these signs near Staple Hall. The point we have mentioned is equally dangerous, and ought to be treated the same way.

****
****
******

E.C. EARLY ELECTED
E.C. Early 346. C. Story 131.

The polling for a U.D.C. Councillor to fill the vacancy created by the resignation of Mr J. Knight took place at the Wesleyan School on Monday 30th August. The day passed off without any excitement. Although the register of voters contains 831 names only 477 recorded their votes. Electors were left pretty much to themselves. There was no systematic canvass, and the only method provided for most of the voters to reach the polling station was on "Shanks's pony". This very natural, but unusual way of arriving at the polling station, combined with the fact that there is no contentious question before the Council at the present time, probably accounts for the small number of electors who exercised their vote.

CHANGE OF DIET

At the meeting of the Guardians of the Witney Union Workhouse Dr Kelly reported that sometime ago the inmates objected to soup for dinner; many of them preferred bread and cheese. The Master now reported that he had ascertained that out of 53 men only 20 preferred soup and out of 33 women only three were in favour of soup. The diet was ordered to be changed in accordance with the wishes of the majority.

JOURNEY TIME CUT

The new Atlantic port at Fishguard has lessened the time from London to New York by 5 hours. What would our grandfathers have said if they had been told that the distance between London and New York would be done in a little under 5 days and 7 hours?

ARE WE AT WAR?

Thousands of troops have passed through the streets of Witney, and all around us fighting has been going on with a fierceness that is almost realistic, and under conditions as rigorous as that which is associated with real warfare.

Some four thousand men of the Royal Artillery, the Army Service Corps and the Irish and Scotch regiments rode through the town to the camp at Sherbourne. The sight was indeed a stirring one, a scene that will not easily be forgotten by the inhabitants. He must be a poor specimen of an Englishman who did not feel proud of our Army as he watched this unusual sight.

A still grander sight was seen when for several hours troops poured into the camp at Park Farm, drenched with rain it is true but exhibiting the same happy spirit that characterised their comrades on the previous Saturday.

On Monday evening of the 20th an incident happened in Witney reminding the inhabitants that "war" was going on in the neighbourhood. An attempt was made to capture five Blue enemies, who had the audacity to enter Red territory. On going down Corn Street they saw a couple of Reds and thinking many more were close at hand, at once turned back and galloped down the street, followed by the two Reds, one of which fell near the Institute. He, however quickly remounted and the race was continued; but the Blues had a good start and succeeded in evading capture by riding into Coggs Wood. The incident caused a good deal of excitement.

This war has not been without its accidents. A severe thunderstorm was responsible for more than one accident. An officer and five men were struck by lightning at Burford: it was earlier reported that the officer had died, but fortunately this has proved to be wrong.

An Army contractor was riding his bicycle along Corn Street when the lightning frightened some horses attached to a baggage wagon, who ran into the cyclist throwing him to the ground, the wagon passed over his body. He was picked up unconscious and removed to a house close at hand, where he remained in the same condition for several days. The unfortunate man is still in a very critical state.

Everybody is asking the question – "Will the troops remain over Sunday?" It is impossible to say, the secret of their future movement is strictly guarded. All we know for certain is that "war" begins again on Monday, and continues incessantly till Wednesday, when the manœuvres close.

ELEMENTARY SCHOOLS CLOSED

Owing to the continuance of the whooping cough epidemic it has been decided to close the elementary schools of the town for another fortnight till Monday October 11th.

WITNEY WEST DISTRICT

Mr. Powell reported as follows:–
Army Manœuvres – Before the Army Manœuvres began I made an inspection of all roads and bridges in the district and submitted a report to the County Surveyor. As soon as possible after the manœuvres I again made an inspection of roads etc., and again submitted a report as to the damage done with an estimate of costs. With respect to the district roads, there was no damage done; but some of the guardrails along the road at Kelmscot and Grafton were broken and also a hole was made in the bridge on the Langley road. This bridge is constructed with iron "Tee" rails about two foot nine inches apart, and covered with two-inch planks. On the West side a couple of planks gave way. I took Mr. Horne the wheelwright of Clanfield around with me. He submitted an estimate to do the necessary repairs, which I sent to the Army Manœuvres Compensation Officer who allowed £8 10s. Mr. Horne has now repaired the damage.

A BAD CASE OF CRUELTY

The Master of the Workhouse reported that the police had brought in a child who had evidently been ill-treated. The child was four years old, but could not walk and was covered with bruises. The child's teeth were bleeding, probably from a blow in the mouth, and it had two black eyes. The woman from whom the child was taken is to be prosecuted.

INCREASED EXPENDITURE

The half-yearly returns have now been completed and are in the hands of the Guardians. The Chairman said that they would find that Witney was the highest Union in the County for the half-year, having increased expenditure by £157 for in and out maintenance. He believed a large portion of that extra expenditure was due to the extra 1/- and 6d given to old people last winter. Dr. Macray thought the money was well spent. Mr. M. Florey asked whether other Unions did not do the same thing. The Chairman replied that he believed they did not.

WITNEY ORCHESTRAL SOCIETY

At the A.G.M. of the Society the Chairman (Mr. W. H. Tarrant) referred to the progress the Society had made under the able conductorship of Mr. H. W. Sprenger. A suggestion that some concrete appreciation of Mr. Sprenger's services should be made, had met with unanimous and enthusiastic support of the members. This had taken the form of a pair of silver candlesticks. Mr. Sprenger thanked them very much for their handsome present and said it had come as a complete surprise to him. The object of the Society was to bring together the instrumentalists of the town and district in order to study good music, and afterwards to give a public concert that otherwise could not be heard outside the larger towns.

BREAD AND BEEF

An important matter for Witney people was brought forward at the Bailiff's Feast, when reference was made to the proposed alterations in the distribution of the charities. For some years there has been a growing feeling that something should be done to bring about a better state of things.

The most abused has been the Bread and Beef Charity. The reason for this is not far to seek; fresh Bailiffs are elected each year, and both of them being new to the work abuses have crept in, until the present time we are ashamed to say four-fifths of the inhabitants partake of the charity. Instances can be given of families whose aggregate earnings amount to over £4 a week, and at Christmas time they are included in the list of the "poor" who receive bread and beef. In this list are people with small families whose wages amount to £2 or £3 a week.

Two schemes have been evolved. The larger is to pool the charities and bring them under the control of a body of trustees, while the lesser scheme is for a thorough revision of the bread and beef distribution.

WITNEY CHARITIES

The scheme to pool the charities of the town is before the Charity Commissioners. One can readily see what an immense boon to the town the pooling of this £350 of charity money would be, instead of different sets of trustees distributing this money in their own particular way. Each case would be dealt with on its merits, and in a way best suited to the needs of the applicant. A charity should be distributed in such a way as to give the best possible results, and how can this be attained by insisting upon giving a man a pair of boots, when his more urgent need is a suit of clothes, we fail to see. All this could be adjusted under the larger scheme.

We congratulate the Bailiffs and those working with them, on the plucky attempt they are making to consolidate the charities.

To the Editor of the Witney Gazette,

Sir, We gladly take this opportunity of making public the improvements which we hope to effect in the method of distribution of the Witney Charities. The deeds which relate to the Witney and Freeland Trusts state that the money is left for the "use of the poor of the town of Witney", at the discretion in the one case of the Bailiffs, in the other of the Rector, Bailiffs, churchwardens and overseers. There is no mention in any bequest of the charity taking the form of bread and beef except in that of William Lee, who assigned forty shillings to be spent at Christmas on forty poor men and women, twopence on bread and ten pence on beef, with three shillings and fourpence for a drink for the Burgesses. As trustees of a charity,

we feel very strongly that in whatever manner this money is given away it ought only to be distributed to the poor, and that whatever is given to those who are not poor is taken from those who are in greater need.

Among other plans the providing of a Cottage Hospital, and a fund for dealing with special cases of distress and necessity appear particularly worthy of attention.

We are, yours truly,
Chas. E. M. Kelly } *Bailiffs of*
C. Story } *Witney*

The Editor, *"Witney Gazette"*

Sir, – I think it is the duty of every working man, and tradesman, to oppose any alteration of distribution. If you will allow me, I should also like to say that, when reading the account of the Bailiff's Feast I was surprised to note the large number of recipients, and guests of the very gentlemen who advocate putting the cost of the working man's Christmas dinner to other use. Has it ever occurred to the Bailiffs that the cost of such a feast was a waste of money? I note also in the speeches one Bailiff says so many of the population suddenly become poor at Christmas. I should like to suggest that any gentleman who thinks the working man is not already poor should try for twelve months living on the average working man's wage, and I think he will find himself suddenly poor, and poorer still at Christmastime, when work is slack, a short week, and money most needed. I will conclude my letter by telling the Bailiffs if their plot succeeds they will have the comforting satisfaction of knowing that they have deprived many a home of a good Christmas dinner.

Yours truly,
A Witney Man.

EDUCATION

At the Witney Science School, Mr Boulter gave a lecture to teachers on the education of children.

**

He said that in order to give the child the best education there must be good teachers. The craze for economy had not eliminated from schools the unqualified teacher, but he thought that the time was not far distant when every class was taught by properly qualified teachers. Smaller classes were also necessary to efficient education. The N.U.T. put the maximum class size at 40.

**

In large towns parents, to a large extent, seemed to think that teachers had taken the place of the parent entirely, but what they as teachers had to do was to impress upon parents their responsibility. They had to show them that they must work hand in hand with the teacher if the child's education was to be efficient. A child's character was formed to a certain extent at school, but to a much greater extent at home.

**

Jottings comments,

The lack of authority over children in the home is causing great anxiety amongst educationalists at the present time. When a boy commences to work for a living, he has escaped the discipline of school life, and he at once attempts to show his independence at home. Instead of checking him, his parents allow him to do pretty well what he likes, and the boy instead of improving his position by study lapses into careless habits, and probably becomes an idle man, or, if it is possible, something worse. It is this parental neglect of children when they have reached their teens,

that has done much to swell the ranks of the hooligans and the unemployable.

**

The young of England will have to guide the ship of state through the troubled waters of the future, in the hands of the children of to-day will be placed the national responsibility of tomorrow. Mr. Boulter emphasised the importance of developing the body as well as the mind. In the future the two will undoubtedly go together, for we want to see the rising generation a robust and happy race, and that can never be unless the teacher is allowed to devote more attention to the physical needs of the children than he does at the present time.

**

Mr. Boulter is old–fashioned enough to believe in a thorough grounding in the Three "R's". It has been the fashion for well nigh a generation to pay scant attention to this important point. He calls it the foundation of education. What failure there has been in the past has been to a large extent due to children not having learnt sufficiently these rudiments of education.

St. MARY'S CHURCH OF ENGLAND GIRLS SCHOOL

An interesting competition took place, in connection with the above school. A certain number of girls were given one shilling, with which they each had to provide, and afterwards to cook a dinner. All their efforts were most successful, and reflect the greatest credit on the cookery instructress Miss Johnson. Prizes were won by M. Godfrey and W. Talbot 1st. Gladys Thomas and F. Bourton 2nd. The necessary shillings and prizes were provided by the Rev. C. W. O. and Mrs. Jenkyn.

BREAD AND BEEF

The Bailiffs of Witney have distributed some £110 worth of beef and about £20 worth of bread. The method of distribution, which we understand is highly appreciated by the recipients, has been by means of tickets enabling holders to select their own beef, and it has the additional advantage of economy, inasmuch as the cost of distribution this year amounts to a little over 1 per cent as against 15 per cent in previous years.

1910

The General Election did not produce a conclusive result, though in Mid-Oxon it did produce a new Member of Parliament. Mr Asquith continued to press for an end to the House of Lords' power of veto, which had blocked the 1909 Budget and left many Liberal Government plans in disarray. The second Election of the year, in December, resulted in a dead heat and intensified the battle between Commons and Lords. It was not until August 1911 that the Peers reluctantly gave up the fight.

The Suffragettes were stepping up their campaign, but making little progress.

With the rest of the nation, Witney mourned King Edward VII and welcomed King George V and Queen Mary, who led a traditional Royal life through a reign which was to see not only enormous advances in technology and improvements to everyday life, but also the unimaginable horror and bloodshed of the Great War.

EXPLOSION AT THE BREWERY

On December 27th at about 9.30am, an explosion occurred at the Eagle Brewery. The office was totally wrecked, and its contents strewn about the yard. It is thought that an undetected escape of gas was the cause, eventually finding vent when the office was closed for the holidays.

NO MUD HERE

The muggy weather we have been having has been very trying for the roads. All round this district the highways have been lanes of mud, and horses have been slipping and sliding in all directions, while cyclists have experienced some of the perils of riding a two-wheel machine. In the midst of all this mud Witney streets have been carefully swept and kept beautifully clean. We congratulate the Witney U.D.C.'s Surveyor on the excellent state of our streets, which cannot fail to have been much appreciated by those who use them.

MINISTER'S DEATH

It is our painful duty to report the death of the Rev. W.H. Walker, at the age of 66 years. He first came to Witney in 1883 as second Wesleyan minister, later becoming superintendent. After many years of active ministry in the North, he returned to Witney 13 years ago in indifferent health, as a supernumerary. He still worked energetically for the Wesleyan Church, founding the Lowell's Place Adult School and becoming honorary secretary to the Witney branch of the Bible Society. His kindness, generosity and broad-mindedness made for him many friends outside his own communion.

OLD FOLKS' REUNION

The Wesley Guild, who are mostly young people, gave their annual treat and reunion to the old folk of Witney, 106 of whom sat down to an enjoyable repast at 6.45. Three hearty cheers were given for the pensioners, of whom there were quite a score or more, the oldest person being 86. About fifty of the most aged were brought and taken home in conveyances.

CHILDREN'S COURT

Previous to the Petty Sessions a Children's Court was formed to hear charges of wilful damage to an iron fence against two boys aged eleven and one of nine. They pleaded guilty and were fined 2/6d each and put on Probation for 12 months.

A WITNEY LAD'S HEROISM

At the annual 'social' of the 1st Witney Company Boys' Brigade, Lance-Corporal F.S. Richardson was presented with a Royal Humane Society Certificate for saving the life of a little boy named Weller, who got into difficulty while bathing in deep water at 'Tognall', part of the river Windrush. Though suffering from a strained arm Richardson plunged in and, swimming on his back, managed to get him to the bank in spite of his struggles.

FANCY COSTUME DANCE

A very successful dance was held by the Church of England Men's Society. At the children's dance in the afternoon J. Barnes won first prize dressed as 'a real Witney blanket'.

THE DAYLIGHT COMET

Many people in Witney have recently had a very good view of the daylight comet. On the nights of Friday the 22nd and Saturday the 23rd it was seen to great advantage about 6 o'clock. The tail on Saturday evening was about 5 degrees long, and very conspicuous. On both nights it was seen for about three quarters of an hour.

SIGNALS ERECTED

We are glad to be able to record that, thanks to the Witney U.D.C., these signals have now been erected: on the east side of Church Green, near the Church, a danger signal bearing the words, 'Please drive slowly'; similar signals are to be found at the bottom of Corn Street, at the dangerous corner near the bleach house, Mill Street, and in Newland, opposite the cricket field. Ordinary standard signals have been erected at the Goods Station corner, and on Wood Green near Costal Farm.

ELECTION SPECIAL

MID-OXON CONSTITUENCY

Candidates: the sitting Member, Mr E.N. Bennett (Lib.) and Mr A. St.G Hamersley (Con.)

ELECTION ADDRESSES

MR BENNETT said of the Liberals, quoting Mr Henderson, the Labour Party leader, that 'No Government has ever done so much for the workers'. The Liberals had successfully established a system of Old Age Pensions, but many great measures had been destroyed by the House of Lords; it had even refused to pass the Budget. It was intolerable that a Second Chamber should act simply as a wing of the Tory party. Reform was needed. The principle of 'One Man, One Vote' must be established and plural votes abolished. He was unalterably opposed to 'Tariff Reform'. As Parliamentary Private Secretary to the new Secretary for Agriculture, he would at all times be glad to further the interests of farmers. He was in favour of the Enfranchisement of Women.

MR HAMERSLEY said that he was determinedly opposed to leaving the country in the hands of a single Chamber. The Lords were right to ask the people if they wanted a revolutionary and Socialistic Budget. He supported Tariff Reform, which would secure fair play for British trade and Workmen by preventing the dumping in this country of the products of foreign sweated labour. Land Laws and the Poor Law should be reformed and all undesirable aliens excluded from our shores. He stressed the slogan *'BRITAIN FOR THE BRITISH'*.

POLLING DAY

Not a little excitement was manifested in Witney on polling day, Friday, Jan. 21st. At an early hour motors were astir, and voters were brought up to the polling station in good time. Both parties were well provided with vehicles, and this probably accounted for the fact that 90% of voters on the Witney register came to the poll. Many people enjoyed their first ride in a motor car, but there were some who looked with suspicion on these modern vehicles, and in some villages voters preferred to walk rather than use a motor. Soon after midday, Mr E.N. Bennett visited his committee room in the Market Square, and received a hearty reception from his supporters. About 3 o'clock Mr Hamersley motored in and visited his committee room at the Town Hall, where he met with an enthusiastic reception. All day the streets were enlivened with crowds of people wearing their favourite colours, and a considerable amount of good-natured bantering went on. Three of the oldest inhabitants recorded their vote; their ages were 97, 92 and 92. This we should think establishes a record. Polling day was singularly free from accidents, the only one being a motor smash at Hailey, the car, which was considerably damaged, running into a wall, but fortunately the driver, the only occupant, escaped without injury.

THE RESULT

On Saturday, outside the Post Office, the news of Mr Hamersley's victory by a majority of 720 was cheered by a large crowd of supporters.

Woodeaton, Islip. Oxon.
Jan. 24th, 1910
To all Supporters of the Unionist cause in the Woodstock Parliamentary Division of Oxfordshire.
Please accept my heartfelt thanks for the help you have given and the hard work you have done, so largely contributing thereby to our great victory.
A. St. G. HAMERSLEY

To the Electors of Mid-Oxfordshire,
GENTLEMEN,-
I wish to express my sincere thanks to all my friends in Mid-Oxfordshire who during this Election have supported the Liberal cause by their votes and work. We Liberals, at any rate, have no cause for self-reproach as regards the conduct of our campaign, for we fought on straightforward and honourable lines. Never was any Candidate better served than I was by the unselfish work and devotion of his friends. I am deeply grateful for the numerous expressions of sympathy and encouragement which have reached me from friends in all parts of the Division, most of them men and women in humble circumstances, who, sometimes at the risk of personal loss to themselves, have bravely ranged themselves on the side of our good cause. Under any system of electoral fair-play, Mid-Oxfordshire is, I am convinced, a Liberal constituency, but for the moment the efforts of our Liberals in the Division have been neutralised by the cruel handicap of the 'plural voter'.
E.N. BENNETT
Oxford,   Jan. 25th, 1910.

COMETS AND THEIR HISTORY

A most interesting talk on Comets was given at the Girls' Club House by the Rev. C.R.N. Blakison, illustrated by lantern slides ably manipulated by the Rev. A.S.C. Austen. This was the first of a series of lectures to be given on scientific and literary subjects, proceeds to go to the New Church House Fund.

COMING OF AGE

The employees of Messrs. Pritchett & Co, Newland, were entertained at the 'Fleece' Hotel, on the occasion of the coming of age of Mr H. Norman Pritchett. Tea was provided for the women, followed by a dinner for the men, the catering for both being ably carried out by Mr F. Moore. During the evening the employees presented a handsome solid silver inkstand, together with a meerschaum pipe, to Mr Norman Pritchett, who ably acknowledged the gifts.

WANTED - LANDLESS MEN FOR MANLESS LAND.
Intending Emigrants for Canada should book through H.T. TITCOMB, 9 CORN STREET, WITNEY, and save themselves all trouble and worry.
**NOW IS THE TIME.
INFORMATION FREE.**

A TRIVIAL CASE

The Court was crowded when Frederick John Wyatt, schoolmaster, was summoned by Joseph Clements for assaulting his son, William Clements, at Hailey.

Clements said that he had found marks on the boy's neck and lumps on his head. The doctor had found three slight abrasions on the left buttock. However, several teachers and pupils gave evidence that they had seen Mr Wyatt cane the boy on the hand and shake him by the collar, but nothing else. For the defence, Mr Cuthbert said the case should never have been brought. Clements had admitted he had a conscientious objection to corporal punishment, but this was allowed by the law. He submitted that the punishment was moderate and reasonable. The Chairman dismissed the case, saying the Bench did not think the child had been unduly punished (applause).

WORKHOUSE DEATHS

Between February 15th and the 23rd, there were five deaths at the Union Workhouse: William Shirley, 90 years; Edwin Kitchener, 79; Hannah Minchin, 79; Maria Harrod, 81, and Eliza Thornet, 90.

MILL STREET WIDENED

One of the greatest improvements that has been carried out in Witney for many years is the widening of Mill Street. In these days of motors, the narrow entrance from the Bridge end was a veritable death-trap. Now that the slum houses on the south side of the street have been pulled down and replaced by modern villas, and the road widened to 30 feet, one wonders why some steps were not made years ago to bring about such a desirable state of things.

WHIST DRIVE

Some 140 persons attended a very successful whist drive in aid of the New Church House fund. The large hall of the Corn Exchange was transformed into a most comfortable room, being well warmed with stoves and attractively draped with flags. Refreshments were served, and Ladies' and Gentlemen's prizes were presented by Mrs Kirby.

NOTICE TO FARMERS: Owing to the abnormally wet season, MESSRS. PHILLIPS & SONS are prepared to DRY CORN, on their kiln at Witney, at 2/- per quarter. Application should be made to Mr W.G. Phillips, The Hill, Witney.

SECOND LECTURE

'Oliver Goldsmith' was the subject of the second lecture at the Girls' Club House. The speaker was Dr. Kelly.

NURSING ASSOCIATION

Many towns the size of Witney have cottage hospitals. Our blanket town is without this boon, but it has got the next best thing - a Nursing Association, which some years ago was placed upon a non-sectarian footing. For some inexplicable reason, it is not supported so well as it deserves. Subscriptions, fees from private patients, collections and donations bring the receipts up to £76-13-7d. How the Association can pay a Nurse and meet other expenses within this narrow margin is a mystery. It is conducted in a business-like and economical manner, but more means of relief to sufferers could be procured if more finance were available. We feel sure Witney people only need to have these facts before them, and they will support the Nursing Association in a manner worthy of the best traditions of the town. We are informed that Nurse Scudamore, of 39 The Crofts, has just been appointed as Nurse by the Association.

SWITZERLAND LECTURE

The Rev. A.S. Austen gave a lantern lecture on 'Switzerland' at the Girls' Club House. He spoke of the patriotism of the Swiss, their habits and their system of education. The views were shown by Mr Adams, who kindly lent his lantern.

NEW M.P. IN WITNEY

Mr A. St.G. Hamersley, newly-elected M.P. for the constituency, attended a crowded smoking concert organised by the Witney Conservative Association. This took place only a few days after he had made his maiden speech in the Commons, in which he deplored the importation of foreign hops. He failed to see why labour should not be protected in this country against the competition of Chinese and coloured men.

BOYS' BRIGADE SALE

The members of the 1st Witney Company, the Boys' Brigade, (kindly assisted by several lady friends) conducted a rummage sale at the Wesleyan Schools, when the substantial sum of £8 was raised in aid of the Company funds. This, their first effort, having proved a success, the members have decided to make the event an annual affair.

NOTICE!

Whereas it having come to my knowledge that certain persons have been circulating an accusation with regard to my wife being the originator of a certain scandal, which is without foundation, proceedings will be taken against anyone repeating the same after this date.
(Signed) A. NICKLEN, Newland, Witney.
March 18th, 1910.

SOLDIERS' FOOTBALL FIASCO

The match between Witney Town and the 7th Company, Aldershot Depot, Army Service Corps ended in a 5-1 win for Witney. The very unpropitious weather discouraged many spectators from attending, and those who did were not rewarded with a worthy display. From their arrival in the town it was manifest that the soldiers were out for a merry-making holiday; they appeared to treat the occasion in a manner void of very earnest intentions.

APOLOGY

This is to certify that I have accused the wife of Mr A. Nicklen as being the originator of a scandal. I regret having done so, and humbly apologise for the inconvenience caused thereby.
(Signed) CLARA SOWERBY, Newland, Witney
March 23rd, 1910.

TOLLGATE OUTDATED

The question arises of doing away with the tollgate at Eynsham. We believe that it is the unanimous opinion that this relic of bygone days, when our ancestors took things more easily than we do, should be abolished.

In these days of motors, and the increasing value of time, a toll gate is just a public nuisance. Surely the County Council could pay a lump sum to the owner to stop charging tolls. The longer they delay, the bigger will be the bill.

SAD DEATH OF DR. KELLY

It is our painful duty to record the death of Dr. Kelly, of Staple Hall, at the early age of 45. He was a man of brilliant attainments and genial disposition who found time for public work in the midst of his arduous medical duties. He was Senior Bailiff of Witney as well as Deputy Coroner and Medical Officer to the Witney Union Workhouse. An inquest heard that he had been suffering from acute stomach pains, for which he injected himself with an overdose of morphia. The Jury returned as verdict of death by misadventure.

MRS CHARLES KELLY, CANON and MRS KELLY and FAMILY desire to express their thankfulness for the warm expressions of sympathy and tokens of affection which they have received on all sides during their late and sad bereavement.

WITNEY NURSING ASSOCIATION

During March Nurse Scudamore paid 195 visits to the sick. She has received presents of old linen from the Parish Council and from Holy Trinity Church, but is still in want of more. She is also in want of a water ring. Will some kind friend present one to the Association? The cost would be about 15/-. It has come to the knowledge of the Committee that some people are afraid to ask for the services of the Nurse lest they should forfeit their right to an Old Age Pension. It cannot be stated more clearly that the services of the Nurse in no way disqualify anyone for an Old Age Pension.

TO LET - The 'ANGEL INN', Market Place, Witney; fully licensed; early possession may be had. Apply, Church & Co., Ltd., Eagle Brewery, Witney.

BOYS BRIGADE IN OXFORD

On Easter Monday the members of the 1st Witney Company, the Boys' Brigade, marched to the station and boarded the 12.28 train to Oxford. Their first visit was to the Martyrs' Memorial and the flat cross in the roadway indicating the spot where the martyrs were burned to death. They then visited several Colleges, the old City's fortified wall, the Botanic Garden, Tom Tower, and finally the tea-house, where justice was done to an ample supply. They returned by the 7pm train in jolly spirits, having spent 'a rattling good time', and heartily thanked their officers for so kindly organising the outing.

WITNEY SPORTS

Excellent weather conditions prevailed at the Easter Sports, which were attended by over 3000 people. The horse races were far from exciting, as one animal, 'Undecided', was far superior to any of the others. The athletic events were well contested, but the long waits between races still provoke adverse criticism. If the fixture is to maintain its popularity, there will have to be some improvement in this direction.

FOOTBALL INCIDENT

In the second half of the match between the Cygnets and the Harriers (Witney and District League), a player who had been warned for misconduct addressed the referee, Mr Ford, in unparliamentary language. When ordered off he refused to go, in spite of his Captain's requests. The referee's only course of action was to leave the ground and abandon the match. We are glad to hear that he upheld his authority in this way. Football depends for its popularity on the game being played in a proper and sportsmanlike manner. The player was later suspended by the Oxford Football Association until December 1910.

WOOL FAIR PROPOSAL

A public meeting was held on April 14th to discuss a suggestion that Witney should be the centre for an annual wool fair. Those attending decided to ask the Fat Stock Committee to take the matter in hand, and to form a sub-committee to arrange details. The project deserves the support of all who have the welfare of the district at heart, and to the woollen manufacturers it must commend itself from a purely business point of view.

MUFFLED PEAL

A quarter peal of Stedman Triples (1260) was rung on the bells of the Parish Church, in 47 minutes, in memory of a former ringer, Mr E. Baker, of Ducklington, who was buried at Witney on the same day.

FOR SALE - A WOODEN BUILDING, suitable for anyone obliged to sleep in the open air. 'M', Gazette Office, Witney.

GAS FOR NEWLAND?

The question of a gas supply for Newland was discussed by Coggs Parish Council. One wonders the matter has not been brought up before. Here in Witney for half a century we have been using gas, and the inhabitants of Newland, living only a few yards away, have had to be content with oil as an illuminant. It is time this convenience was made possible by the Parish Council.

TWO GOVERNESS CARS for sale, with Rubber Tyred Wheels; also PONY CART, cheap. T. Burgess, Ducklington.

NOTICE: next term, the School which has been formerly conducted by the MISSES EARLY, will be carried on by the MISSES WALKER at 39 HIGH STREET, WITNEY. Pupils will receive a thoroughly modern education, with preparation for the Oxford Local Examinations, if desired. Languages and Music are specialities.

BOY SCOUTS FOR WITNEY

We are glad to note that arrangements are being made to form a local organisation of Boy Scouts in Witney. The town has plenty of material for forming an excellent detachment, and we hope that the idea will be well supported by those who have the interests of the lads at heart.

NEW MEDICAL OFFICER

The Board of Guardians has unanimously appointed Mr C.P. Harvey as medical officer and public vaccinator for the Witney Union Workhouse and district, in the place of the late Dr Kelly.

FIRE-LIGHTERS - A Shilling Packet will light 100 fires. Knight Bros., 20, High Street, Witney.

BIRTH
MOSS-HOLLAND - May 14th, at the 'Three Horse Shoes' Inn, Corn Street, the wife of J. Moss-Holland, a daughter.

LOST- On Thursday evening, from trap, between Witney and Minster Lovell, a white-handled CARVING FORK. Anybody returning it to the Gazette Office will be rewarded.

DEATH OF KING EDWARD VII

THE OFFICIAL ANNOUNCEMENT

"Buckingham Palace, May 6th, 1910, 11.50pm.
His Majesty the King breathed his last at 11.45 tonight in the presence of Her Majesty Queen Alexandra, the Prince and Princess of Wales, the Princess Royal (Duchess of Fife), the Princess Victoria and Princess Louise (Duchess of Argyll).
F.H. LAKING, M.D.,
JAMES REID, M.D.,
DOUGLAS POWELL, M.D.,
BERTRAND DAWSON, M.D."

WITNEY'S SYMPATHY
The following telegram was sent to His Majesty George V:
"We, the Bailiff of the ancient borough of Witney and the members of the Witney Urban District Council, tender our loyal and sincere sympathy with your Gracious Majesty and the members of the Royal Family in your great loss.
C. Story, Bailiff, E. Tarrant, Chairman."

THEIR MAJESTIES' THANKS

Mr. Story and Mr. Tarrant received the following reply:
"Their Majesties sincerely thank you, and the Chairman and members for their kind telegram.
Equerry."
A similar message was sent to Queen Alexandra by the 'Garibaldi' Lodge of Oddfellows, and received a gracious reply.

SCOUTS UNDER CANVAS

The Scouts of the 1st Witney Company, The Boys' Brigade, and the newly-formed 1st Witney and District Troop of the Baden-Powell Scouts, both spent Whitsuntide under canvas. The Boys' Brigade were encamped at a high spot between New Mill and Crawley. In spite of having sentries posted, they were attacked and defeated in the early hours of Monday morning by the Baden-Powell Scouts, who executed a clever stratagem for which their opponents congratulated them. Their camp was at Handborough. Fire-lighting, Church Parade and bathing took place as well as tracking, message-carrying and other exciting activities. The lads all agreed that it was a jolly good holiday.

FIRST-CLASS NEW PUNT for sale. Apply Long & Berry, Builders, West End, Witney.

THE KING IS DEAD LONG LIVE THE KING

OUR BURFORD COMMENTATOR writes: The late King Edward was a great man, a man with very great knowledge, derived not from books, but from personal interviews with those who write books. He was, as the late Mr. Gladstone said, 'a very clever and well-informed man.' He looked a King indeed. A friend of mine who had the honour of speaking to him for a few minutes upon one occasion was very much surprised to hear his German accent...His son King George the Fifth has taken his father's place with such order, and with the display of such enthusiasm, as would have been well nigh impossible under the circumstances with any other people in Europe...His will be no bed of roses, but a task the nature of which almost makes the mind reel...

CHURCH SERVICES

Special services were held in the Churches of Witney.

OUR SOVEREIGN LORD KING GEORGE V

PROCLAMATION OF KING GEORGE V

The Proclamation Ceremony took place on Tuesday, May 10th, at 12.30.

The procession was formed at Staple Hall as follows: Mounted Constable (P.C. Seymour). Witney Town Band, led by Mr A. Smith. Mace Bearer (Mr G. Walker). P.C. Hubbard and P.C. Panting. The Bailiff of Witney (Mr C. Story). Chairman of Urban District Council (Mr E. Tarrant) with the Clerk (Mr. R.F. Cuthbert). Members of the Witney Urban District Council. The Clergy and Ministers. Representatives of the adjoining Councils. Witney Fire Brigade. Residents of Witney. The Friendly Societies.

After a fanfare, the Proclamation was read by Mr Story, mounted on a white horse. The people heartily repeated his cry of 'God Save the King', and the National Anthem followed, led by the Band. Three cheers for the King and a fanfare concluded the ceremony, which was repeated at Parliament House in Corn Street, and at the Town Hall. All the town's schoolchildren were present. The Boys' Brigade and the Boy Scouts acted as marshals. A woman who was seized with hysterics was attended by the ambulance section of the Boys Brigade, assisted by the Scouts, who took her to the Marlborough Hotel, where she soon recovered.

ALEXANDRA THE QUEEN MOTHER

THE DUKE OF CORNWALL

A MAGISTRATE'S LENIENCY

On May 19th, at the Police Court, Burford, Henry Moore and John Foley, labourers, were charged with sleeping in an outhouse at Whitehill Farm, Burford, the same night, and having no visible means of subsistence. The Magistrate, Charles East Esq., took into consideration that this was the first case under the new King, and discharged the defendants with a caution.

IS THIS A RECORD?

King George's accession means that Messrs William Gardner and Thomas Clarke, who were both born in 1813, have now lived in six reigns.

KING GEORGE'S CALL - 'Wake up, England.' Response - English made watches, 5/- each, at DAVIS'S, Watchmaker, High Street, Witney.

Knight's printing works, where the Gazette was printed.

MONEY, WEIGHTS AND MEASURES IN KING EDWARD VII'S TIME

The days of 'l.s.d.' are long gone; the initials even seemed archaic when the currency they represented was in use, for they stand for the Latin words 'librae' (pounds), 'solidi' (gold Roman coins) and 'denarii' (silver Roman coins). Pounds, shillings and pence were the more modern version of these names.

A **POUND** (£) consisted of 20 shillings. There were no pound notes until 1914; a gold coin called a 'sovereign' was used.

A **GUINEA** (£1 1s), one pound one shilling, was much used for shop prices, school fees etc. Sometimes a capital 'G' denoted 'guineas'. There was no guinea coin.

A silver **SHILLING** coin represented 12 pence.

A **FLORIN**, or two-shilling piece, was a large silver coin.

Two shillings and sixpence (2/6) made up **HALF A CROWN**, another large silver coin.

A **CROWN**, 5 shillings (5/-), was the largest silver coin.

Other silver coins were the little **SIXPENCE** and the tiny **THREEPENNY PIECE**, sometimes known as a 'threepenny bit'.

The **PENNY** was the main copper coin.

The **HALFPENNY** (½d), whose value is not hard to guess, was smaller than the penny. It was usually pronounced 'hayp'ny', written colloquially as 'ha'penny'.

The **FARTHING** (¼d), worth a quarter of a penny, was the smallest of the 'coppers'.

The ways people wrote their money and referred to it varied. 2s 6d could also be written 2/6, and was called either two and six, two and sixpence or half a crown. 10s 6d (10/6) was ten and six or (sometimes) half a guinea.

When out shopping you might spend 1s 2½d (one and tuppence ha'penny) at the groceer's. 1½d was sometimes called 'a penny ha'penny', sometimes 'three-ha'pence'. £1 10s was either 'one pound ten' or 'thirty shillings' (30s or 30/-).

Larger sums can be read in a straightforward, though rather longwinded way: £46 11s 4½d would be 'forty six pounds eleven and fourpence ha'penny'.

Metrication was a long way off in the 1900s. **INCHES, FEET** and **YARDS** were used in measuring lengths. An **INCH** is 25.4mm, a **FOOT** (12 inches) is 0.3048m, and a **YARD** (3 feet) is 0.9144m. A **MILE** is 1.609km.

A **BUSHEL** was a capacity measure equal to 4 gallons. **PINTS**, (0.568 litre) **QUARTS** (1.136 litres) and **GALLONS** (4.546 litres) are on their way out in the 21st century.

IMPERIAL WEIGHTS include the **OUNCE**, written oz (28.35 grams), the **POUND**, written lb (16oz or 0.4536 kilo), the **STONE** (14lbs or 6.35 kilos), the **HUNDREDWEIGHT**, written cwt (50.80 kilos) and the **TON** (20cwt or 1.016 tonnes).

A **SCORE** is an archaic weight (20lbs) used in weighing livestock.